Literacy Alive!

DRAMA

PROJECTS

FOR

LITERACY

LEARNING

Judith Ackroyd

Hodder & Stoughton

A MEMBER OF THE HODDER HEADLINE GROUP

The publishers would like to acknowledge the following
contributors:

Jonothan Neelands	Foreword
David Booth	Reading the Stories We Construct Together
Jo Boulton	A Brighter Colour for the Literacy Hour
Paul Bunyan	Calling Across the Sea
Sue Boshell	Giant Steps in Writing
John Miller	Whoosh, Bang and Whiz!
Michael Flemming	A Highwayman Comes Riding
Helen Nicholson	A Special Kind of Freedom
Joe Winston	The Gargoyles Creep

p 21 from *The Rainbow Fish* by Marcus Pfister (1992), © North-South Books; pp 37–38
from *When My Ship Comes In* by Alan Gibbons (1998), © HarperCollins Publishers; pp
46–47, 50–51 from *Giant* © Juliet and Charles Snape. Reproduced by permission of the
publisher Walker Books Ltd., London; pp 68, 71 from *The Firework Maker's Daughter*,
© Philip Pullman (1995). Extracted from *The Firework Maker's Daughter* by Philip
Pullman, published by Doubleday, a division of Transworld Publishers. All rights
reserved. pp 80–81, 84–85 'The Highwayman' by Alfred Noyes; p 101 'Anancy' by
Andrew Salkey in *Black Poetry* by Grace Nichols (1988), © Blackie; pp 114, 115, 116
Night of the Gargoyles by Eva Bunting (1995), © David Bennett Books Ltd.

Every effort has been made to trace copyright holders of material reproduced in this book.
Any rights not acknowledged here will be acknowledged in subsequent printings if notice
is given to the publisher.

Orders: please contact Bookpoint Ltd, 78 Milton Park, Abingdon, Oxon OX14 4TD. Telephone: (44)
01235 827720, Fax: (44) 01235 400454. Lines are open from 9.00–6.00, Monday to Saturday, with
a 24 hour message answering service. Email address: orders@bookpoint.co.uk

British Library Cataloguing in Publication Data
A catalogue record for this title is available from The British Library

ISBN 0 340 75774 4

First published 2000
Impression number   10 9 8 7 6 5 4 3 2 1
Year   2005 2004 2003 2002 2001 2000

Copyright © 2000 Judith Ackroyd

Cover photo from Robert Battersby
Typeset by Fakenham Photosetting Limited, 16 Garrood Drive, Fakenham, Norfolk NR21 8NN
Printed in Great Britain for Hodder & Stoughton Educational, a division of Hodder Headline Plc, 338
Euston Road, London NW1 3BH by J.W. Arrowsmiths Ltd, Bristol

Contents

For Andy, Toby, Rupert
– the best

Foreword – Live Language

In editing this collection, Judith Ackroyd has recognised the need to re-define the relationship between drama and literacy in the light of the National Literacy Strategy and the debate about how best to teach literacy in the primary years. She has carefully selected an interesting mix of experienced teachers with the voices of those taking their first steps into teaching. The collection is woven into a coherent whole by the common format of each case study. There is a carefully framed introduction and a concluding section of the book which sets the agenda and draws out from the case studies a clear set of guidelines and principles for teachers to use in their own planning. This selection will provide the basis for our future understanding of the vital relationship between the systems of the English language and the ways in which it is used in both literary experiences and everyday conversations.

At the heart of this collection of classroom-based case studies lies an encounter between the everyday experience of the classroom and the planned curriculum of national policy makers. The National Literacy Strategy (NLS) is a plan to raise standards of literacy in schools in England and Wales. It sets out the required objectives for literacy from Year 1 to Year 7. It provides a detailed map of what children are expected to know and be able to use in literacy. For the policy makers, the literacy curriculum for children is this plan of sequenced objectives neatly laid out in splendid documents.

For teachers in classrooms, however, the curriculum is different. It is not a curriculum of paper but of living experiences. It is made out of the thousands of day to day interactions with 30 or more children whose needs, desires, cultures and abilities are both different and constantly evolving. It is into this complex, subtle and shifting everyday classroom reality that teachers must introduce and follow the planned curriculum of the policy makers. It is this close and intelligent matching of the planned and the lived in ordinary classrooms, which will inspire the reader of this collection.

The teachers represented here have a shared vision. Yes, after each case study we can see that the checklist of planned objectives within the NLS has been covered, but there is so much more. These are teachers who have understood profound truths about literacy and have discovered and invented ways of teaching literacy that engage and feed from children's everyday realities and concerns.

Through their careful planning of how to make the planned curriculum work in the interests of the children in their classrooms, these teachers clearly demonstrate that literacy is not a technology; it is language *in action*. It makes things happen, it is a means of transforming your world, it is the essential thread that joins cause and effect in human affairs. The children in these pages are being offered an empowering definition of literacy as the ability to *choose* and *use* effectively and appropriately a wide variety of dialects and registers according to the situations that they find themselves in and according to their intentions as communicators in those situations.

The medium for this meeting between the planned and lived experience of the curriculum is provided by drama. Through the use of context, role and the need to resolve the problems at the heart of the drama, children are able to work on literacy in concrete and immediate ways – how else can children look at the relationship between language and context except through drama? But the dramas here offer subtler forms of learning and enrichment too. The imagined worlds, the atmosphere, the encounters with new characters and situations, the teasing out of feelings and concerns about who we are and who we are becoming offer children such a powerful, engaging opportunity not just to learn what language is but to learn what it does; how it shapes our identities, defines our worlds, joins us together and yet also divides us. These young learners are neither being denied the pleasures of literary response, whilst they toil over the 'basic skills', nor offered a language system without any real purpose or reason to use it. As they cover and acquire the objectives of the planned curriculum, they are growing in confidence and understanding; working together collaboratively; being valued as language users and valuing each other. Oh, finally I should add that they are having a lot of fun along the way!

May this book help you to take as much pleasure in your teaching as the contributors have so obviously enjoyed in developing their own practice.

Jonothan Neelands

Introducing Literacy and Drama

'How can I teach spelling through drama?' asked a student teacher.
'Which spellings do you want to teach?'
'The class teacher isn't too keen on me teaching drama. She says I have to teach iar/ear/ ere/are endings. Could you tell me how I do that with drama?'
I was in the mood for a challenge.

> The little girl had never been outside the castle gates before. It was forbidden by her stepmother. She pulled her cloak around her. The wind was cold and the wet of the snow was working its way through her flimsy slippers. She didn't regret having crept out into the chilly evening air. She had always loved animals and to see the deer stuck in the trap was more than she could bear. She had run down the back kitchen stairs and noiselessly stepped through the kitchen gardens and out behind the gardener. The deer now freed, she turned back towards the castle gates. It was getting dark and she was frightened. When she got back to the gate, it was locked. She tried to squeeze beside the huge heavy iron bars. No chance. She was locked out. The gardener had left and she was outside the castle grounds.
>
> As she stood on her tip-toes to inspect the lock, she saw a strange key pad. The keys had letters on them. With a gasp of relief, she remembered that there was a password! She had heard it whispered. The password rhymed with 'hair'. If only she could remember what it was.

At this point the children are asked to help the girl. The teacher takes the role of the girl and mimes typing words onto the key pad as the children suggest them. When a child suggests *glare*, the little girl asks how to spell it. The children together have a go. If they get it wrong, the girl exclaims, 'Oh, no. It can't be spelt like that because it says "no word". How else could it be spelt?' When the children suggest a correct spelling, the girl repeats it as she types it in, checking they are all sure. Disappointed, she cries, 'Please think of another. It says "not password".'

The children continue to think of words which rhyme with 'hair' for no other reason than wanting to help the poor girl. To keep the tension high, the girl keeps looking over her shoulder. At any moment she might be caught outside the castle grounds. She doesn't know what horrid punishment her stepmother would enforce.

As the words are suggested, they are spelt out. When they are wrong, they are attempted again. It sounds like an old fashioned spelling lesson. So what is the difference? Literacy learning through drama can be literacy taught in disguise! A class simply asked by the teacher to think of rhyming words to spell would know that they were supposed to learn the spellings. Here in the drama the children are engaged in quite another task. They are helping a kind girl who is in trouble. The story is what matters. They are happy to keep trying out words to ensure the girl gets to safety, which of course, when the teacher feels enough words have been covered, she does – 'That's it! You've saved my skin. Oh, thank you. The gate is opening. Look!' The focus is not on having to learn the spellings, it is trying out words to solve the problem. But in order to do so, spellings must be learnt.

What the student teacher who taught this activity discovered is interesting. The children did only slightly better in spelling tests later that week, than they did in tests after a more 'usual' spelling session. However, the participation grids that an observer completed during the two sessions indicate very clearly that oral participation started much earlier in the drama, and was much higher throughout. Most of the children contributed, though less than half contributed voluntarily in the usual spelling activity. Furthermore, the children reported much greater pleasure in the drama lesson.

This is, perhaps, rather an extreme example, but it makes the point that finding a fictional reason for the children to learn literacy makes a significant difference to that learning experience. The literacy areas are taught in disguise as something else! Interestingly, writers on second language acquisition have also identified the value in learning whilst seemingly doing something else. Shuy (1981) argues that research has shown 'that good language learning begins with a function, a need to get something done with language, and moves gradually toward acquiring the forms which reveal that function'. A research project I was involved in at Charles University, Prague with second language learners, confirmed this point. A student explained during an interview, '... you are involved in the situation, in the problem. You want to sort it out. You want to help someone or you want to do something together with other people ...' (Ackroyd & Clark, 1998).

This exactly describes what happened in the spelling session. Krashen, influential for his work on communicative approaches to language learning, explains that students best learn language whilst they are engaged in something else (1987). So learning takes place while doing something else in the pretend in drama. Research into drama and writing records pupils' own reflection that the writing carried out through drama had seemed to be a natural part of the drama activity (Neelands et al. 1993). They were doing what had to be done in the drama. It happened to be writing. In Boshell's chapter in this book, children write letters to learn about formal letter writing. In the children's minds, they are writing letters to put wrongs to right in their fictional world. Another Czech student engaged in drama for language learning recorded, 'If you just sit and write . . . you get bored very easily, but when you are playing in this kind of drama, you somehow don't know you are learning, but you are.' (Ackroyd & Clark, 1998).

The context of this book

'How can I teach spelling through drama?' asked a student teacher. Those outside the United Kingdom may be amazed that this question was asked. Indeed, such a question would not have been asked two years ago here. The National Literacy Strategy has run for one year. It involves a Literacy Hour, the government's all but compulsory daily lesson, prescribing the following:

* 15 minutes on text work involving whole class teaching and writing;
* 15 minutes teacher focus on specific words and sentences;
* 20 minutes individual reading and writing;
* 10 minutes plenary of the lesson.

Research at the end of the first year suggests that teachers are using the guidelines, but flexing them to suit their teaching. (Marshall, 1999.) Concerns that there is not enough time for extended reading and writing are met in some schools by a regular 'collapsing' of the Literacy Hour. However, the pressure is on for schools to operate the hour each morning. The danger here is that once routinised, the delivery becomes arid and dull. This book outlines ways of bringing literacy teaching alive.

David Booth's chapter which opens this book includes his own definition of literacy teaching: 'encouraging the meaning making processes involved with printed text through emotionally connected interactions'. His passionate piece articulates the importance of story in children's learning, and how stories can be used to enable children to create meanings, to understand differences in interpretations, and to identify universals. Here is a writer who has influenced drama worldwide, who has a clear vision of the bounties drama offers children. In the context of the National Literacy Strategy, how are teachers in the UK to hold on to the vision that Booth provides us, and yet deliver what a centrally devised framework prescribes? How can we square this powerful pedagogy with a formal hour of literacy? Many voices in the media are currently seeing no way to do one without the other, that there is no choice but to give up child-centred creative experiences in order to fulfil governmental requirements.

This book seeks to find a way through this dilemma. It is born of a belief that the chasm must and can be bridged. The contributors of this book are committed to holding dear the spirit of Booth's chapter at the same time as being committed to supporting teaching colleagues' delivery of the literacy strategy. So, how is it to be done?

We want a drama that enables children to make choices, decisions and to make sense of the worlds they encounter, yet we must also be mindful of the literacy learning to be delivered. When planning dramas, therefore, it is essential to get the balance right between the pedagogic and the fictional functions of the work, since they are interdependent. If the drama does not engage the children, the motive for literacy learning is lost; if the purpose of the drama in promoting literacy is forgotten, the drama may be valuable but does not deliver the required literacy objectives.

Aims

This book aims to encourage teachers of literacy in any national context to employ drama to enhance the learning possibilities and experiences of children. Clear Lesson Guides are provided for immediate use in the classroom as well as support for those wishing to begin to plan their own dramatic activities. It aims to provide a range of models from those bound up with very specific learning objectives to those concerned with a more holistic approach. The shared classroom experiences are intended to provide exciting and interesting alternatives for practicing teachers. There is a desire to ensure children are empowered by learning to use and manipulate language at the same time as experiencing a range of literary texts.

Contents

When selecting contributors for this book I was determined to include a range of practitioners. Contributors therefore include a student teacher, a class teacher, an advisory teacher and others from higher education. They comprise at one extreme a student inexperienced in the use of drama (who concludes, *if I can do it then anyone can!*), and at the other extreme internationally renowned specialists who have recently applied drama techniques to the teaching of literacy. All work in the United Kingdom, with the exception of David Booth writing from Canada, and have experience in schools since the introduction of the National Literacy Strategy. The different learning, foci and experiences of the authors is evident and provides an interesting richness to the collection. The texts used in the chapters are as varied. There is an ancient poem and a modern one, a novel, picture books, and an 'adult' short story. They cover science fiction, fantasy, historical fiction, and engage multi-cultural considerations.

After Booth's demonstration of the power of drama as a teaching strategy for literacy in its broadest sense, we move on to explore in turn how drama can be used with different age groups. The chapters are arranged in order of the age of the children for whom they are designed, starting with the youngest. They have all been trialed in schools and cover a wide range of literacy objectives. The National Literacy Framework objectives covered are provided in each Lesson Guide. The final chapter draws on the work described in other chapters to consolidate an understanding of three particularly useful dramatic activities, and examines the ways in which they can be employed by readers keen to plan their own drama lessons.

Key Stage	Year	Age
KS1	1	5–6
	2	6–7
	3	7–8
KS2	4	8–9
	5	9–10
	6	10–11

Age group breakdown of Key Stages 1 and 2.

Bibliography

Ackroyd, J. & Clark, U. 'You don't know you're learning, but you are', in *Perspectives*, British Council, Prague, 1998.

Krashen, S. *Principles and Practice in Second Language Acquisition*, Prentice Hall International, 1987.

Marshall, B. *Guardian*, 27 July 1999.

Neelands, J., Booth, D. & Ziegler, S. *Writing in Imagined Contexts: Research Into Drama-Influenced Writing*, Research Services, Toronto Board of Education, 1993.

Shuy, R., 'A Holistic View of Language' in *Research in the Teaching of English*, 15, No 2, pp. 101–111, 1981.

Reading the Stories We Construct Together

°using°

Men are Different – a short story, by Alan Bloch

David Booth is a professor at The Ontario Institute for Studies in Education, University of Toronto, where he teaches literacy and the arts in education. He has written many books on these areas as well as award-winning picture books for children. His work in drama and story has influenced drama teachers worldwide.

Reading on Other Planets

Your mission is to investagate the radioactive astarorid belt orbiting the planet Gamalin-5 for possible mineral resources. You will be taking a type 3 voyager on this mission. It is not very well armed (your wepons are 4 laser canons. Two fixed forword and two on a rotating turet) but it has lots of energy shielding. Two more people will be acopining you. Their names are, Ted Aldwin, and Mark Davides. The fuel batteries on board will have enufe power for 24 days of normel oporation. And the ion fusion prapultion is capabul of propoling your ship at 36 kilapasacals per min. Good luck, Captin.

Curtis and Spenser

A class of primary children from a strong, urban Canadian school, used to working on extended projects, forms the context for this article on literacy and drama. My own work is involved with story and drama, and I was visiting the school to demonstrate for the teachers the effect of working with text using role-play and improvised dialogue.

Because I had not worked with these children before, I chose to read the story aloud to them, and provided copies of the text for the children to use during the drama exploration. My goal was to have the students 'consider a story' – that is, to examine its impact, make connections with their personal worlds, respond to the thoughts of others, and reflect upon the implications of the author's words.

We began with a discussion of robots, drawn from their media experiences, and we listed these on chart paper. Then I read to them the short science fiction story, *Men Are Different*, by Alan Bloch.

Men Are Different

I'm an archaeologist, and Men are my business. Just the same, I wonder if we'll ever find out about Men – I mean *really* find out what made Men different from us Robots – by digging around on the dead planets. You see, I lived with a Man once, and I know it isn't as simple as they told us back in school.

We have a few records, of course, and Robots like me are filling in some of the gaps, but I think now that we aren't really getting anywhere. We know, or at least think the historians say we know, that Men came from a planet called Earth. We know, too, that they rode out bravely from star to star; and wherever they stopped, they left colonies – Men, Robots, and sometimes both – against their return. But they never came back.

Those were the shining days of the world. But are we so old now? Men had a bright flame – the old word is 'divine,' I think – that flung them far across the night skies, and we have lost the strands of the web they wove. Our scientists tell us that Men are very much like us – and the skeleton of a Man is, to be sure, almost the same as the skeleton of a Robot, except that it's made out of some calcium compound instead of titanium. Just the same, there are other differences.

It was on my last field trip, to one of the inner planets, that I met the Man. He must have been the last Man in this system, and he'd forgotten how to talk – he'd been alone so long. Once he learned our language we got along fine together, and I planned to bring him back with me. Something happened to him, though.

One day, for no reason at all, he complained of heat. I checked his temperature and decided that his thermostat circuits were shot. I had a kit of field spares with me, and he was obviously out of order, so I went to work. I turned him off without any trouble. I pushed the needle into his neck to operate the cut-off switch, and he stopped moving, just like a robot. But when I opened him up he wasn't the same inside. And when I put him back together I couldn't get him running again. Then he sort of weathered away – and by the time I was ready to come home, about a year later, there was nothing left of him but bones. Yes, Men are indeed different.

Working in small groups, the children were asked to create 'an instant replay' of the story, without the benefit of a general discussion where they could share their responses. I was able to observe their 'silent' re-enactments, and noticed that all of the ten groups seemed to understand the climax of the plot, where the character of the robot had unfortunately operated on the human, causing his death.

In the follow-up class talk time, the children generally commented on the issue of the robot's attempts to help, without realising the consequences of its actions. They wanted to know who 'the Man' was, why he had travelled to that planet, how the robots had come to control the planet, and if other humans had ever visited the planet. By now the children were deeply inside the text, considering the imagined events, making 'sense' of printed text.

To elaborate upon the story, we, as a group, selected the issue of the Man's origin as the basis for the continued drama exploration. The class had not yet left the text; they were digging into it, mining it, continuing to ask 'what if'. In different small groups, the children brainstormed reasons why 'the Man' might have reached this planet, what the reasons for his visiting the planet could have been, what had caused his 'malfunction'. As the children worked, I interacted with each group from time to time, working in role, asking them to respond to me in role, as they developed their scenarios. Frequently, the children revisited the copies of the text, looking for meaningful cues.

Subsequently, the children gathered in a large circle to observe each of the group's interpretations, and to see how each one added to our collective understanding of the original story. I took part in the dramatisations, as the 'Co-ordinator of Interplanetary Explorations', and questioned and supported each group's role-playing as they presented their projects to the Co-ordinator in order to receive funds for travelling to the planet of robots. Usually one or two children acted as spokespersons and through questioning in role, I was able to involve other group members in the work. They watched each presentation, observing the differences, adding to their story context, and building a greater print world.

The following day, the teacher asked each group of children to retell their proposal plans by writing letters to another teacher, recounting their drama experiences. The following examples demonstrate the language and literacy strength of these young students:

> We're sending 11 people, including you, on a mission to find life on another planet. You will be going for ten days we will give you enough oxygen for 18 days. If you find life, try to observe it and if it hurts you, use the lasers we will give you.
>
> *Alison and Michelle*

> Were sending 1 person. The mission is to get to the disk that they are using on the planet. It holds lots of secret things. Like if they are going to attack

and destroy our planet. It is very important because we need to know. We don't want them to destroy our planet because it is our home. We want to stay alive for along time, so we can change some things.

Evan and Adrienne

We are sending 3 people to an uninhabitied planet. A doctor, a botnest and an astronaught. Their mission is to identify and retreve a certain plant that can be dried and ground up to make an ointment. The ointment will be used to cure a plague. If they do not succeed, they will go to planet 5.0.6.5, to get a subsitute.
They will take with them: 30 days worth of oxygen, 40 days worth of fuel, and enough food for 25 days. Their mission will take 20 days.

Didi and Tommy

Your mission is to go to another planet. One man has bee there before and has never returned. With video tapes we have recived we know the man had landed on the planet. We do not know if this planet holds life. Just in case something deadly lives on this planet we will arm you with dangerous high voltage lazers. If the mission succeeds and you bring back the missing person, you will be paid 10,000 dollars.

Drazen and Billy

Mission: To find a lost colony. Ten people are going with you. The Colony as been gone for over a year now. You have a year and two months. The extra two months is encase of a emergency. You will have weapons encase of a attack.

Elyse and Paula

1.) We have to kill the aliens.
2.) We sent two people on a miossion kill the aliens.
3.) We want the aliens' D.N.A.
4.) You will have oxygen for 20 days and you will go for 10 days.

Mitchell and Justin

The research on intertexuality tells us that we make meaning by connecting the many texts that we have experienced – print texts, life texts, media texts, story texts – constructing newly interwoven stories. These children reveal in their writings, bits and pieces of the books they have read, the television they have seen, the stories they have heard. I was surprised by their choices of words, the scientific terminology, the awareness of trade and commerce, the impact on their burgeoning knowledge base of nationalism and imperialism. The story text we begin with, whether read silently or told aloud, becomes part of the child's meaning making, and as ideas are tried out through interactive responses, the young reader/listener deepens, extends, reconsiders, modifies and reconstructs his or her world view. All of this can happen with each significant literacy experience, supported by teachers who employ drama as a means of expanding the interconnections occurring when children meet a story.

From my own work with children over the years, I have come to recognise the power drama can offer to a story experience. After working with several text selections, in similar activities, children are more likely to explore a story on their own, wondering about the writer's ideas and methods, and wandering among the dozens of text experiences that the story triggers. My personal definition of literacy teaching would involve encouraging the meaning-making processes involved with printed text through emotionally connected interactions. Drama strategies offer us exactly such opportunities.

The Story Imperative

Instead of planning in a vacuum, I usually begin with a story that I know well, and find the power of drama within it. I draw the resources out of the story – its situations, characters, problems, relationships, mood, atmosphere, texture and, especially, its concepts – as a way of stimulating and enriching the children's explorations in drama.

Educator Gavin Bolton (1993) says that the teacher must consider the story from its broadest themes before planning the drama; all questions must prod the children's thinking toward development of universal themes and concepts. The teacher must search for a possible starting point that is relevant to the children's experience and relevant to the spirit of the story. Replaying the story through a literal enactment of the plot may have occasional value, but the teacher should not feel limited to it. Furthermore, the response in these sorts of enactments may be limited to one of memory or recapitulation.

Story drama (Booth, 1994) frees the teacher and children from the pressure of acting out the whole story or remembering a script. Most importantly, the children are allowed to bring what they know to the drama: the drama then engages their imaginations, and they inevitably move closer to the story. In this sense, the drama may even explore the story at one remove through an analogy that unlocks internal comprehension. Because of the brain's ability to use metaphor, it can use the pattern of one set of images to organise quite a different set. Therefore, the images from one story can be used as images for related and yet different meanings. Story drama opens the door to an endless number of linkages in the curriculum.

The Drama Process

In drama, the children are allowed to talk themselves into believing in the fiction of the story, to hear their ideas bounced back, to reframe and refocus their own information and attitudes, to recognise the need for communicating what they believe to those who believe differently, to actually hear their own language at work. Their words sweep them into thought, and as they recognise the truth of what they are saying, that very language is transformed into new patterns. The discourse determines the action, and they see the impact of what has been said, all while they are in the midst of the action, in the eye of the hurricane.

The learning in drama occurs with the experience of being involved directly, so that the students think on their feet as participants. As a teacher, I must move the students into areas of significance where they will be challenged to learn (Wagner, 1999). I cannot detract from their part in shaping the drama, but rather I must build upon it. I can handle decisions concerning styles, strategies and activities, informed by an understanding of the students' needs in a particular situation.

I try to direct their attention not just to the subject of the drama, but to the very language they are using in the drama. As well, I can alter the mode of communication, letting the students argue, inquire, persuade, inform, explain, discuss and reflect. The deeper the drama, the better the potential for language development. I can help children by structuring and limiting the decisions to be made in the drama lesson and by opening the range of options available to them in coping with the situation.

The children gain new understanding about the suitability of language in a particular context. I then have a powerful technique to help them reshape their own knowledge. They can begin to take responsibility for their own learning, influencing the events that occur, as the children and I negotiate our relationships within the drama framework. They begin to spontaneously elaborate on the situation, contributing language and exploring alternate language functions. The initiative to communicate is in the hands of the children, and they have some decision-making power concerning what language is appropriate.

11

The Reading Process

No one 'reads reading'; everyone reads for a purpose (Booth, 1998). Every word is a process, and the reader is as important a part of that process as the text. The reading experience is a personal one: the reader understands what the words say to him or her, translates the experience he or she has read about into his or her own context, and responds with feelings and attitudes about the experience and the text. It is common for teachers to discuss the knowledge relevant to a text (awareness of the source, the author, traditions and techniques). However, not much time has been devoted to those qualities that the reader brings to the text (feelings, experiences, attitudes, values and beliefs).

Meanings are constructed through one's total life experience and no more by reading instruction than in any other way. To derive full comprehension, a reader must become the co-author, absorbing the concepts presented and then scrutinising and assessing those ideas in the light of his or her own knowledge and experience. What accounts for the understanding a reader is able to bring to bear on a story at any given moment are experiences between readings – warm-ups and follow-ups that help him or her to grasp a text better when alone with it. What is needed for good comprehension are strong motivation before reading and strong intellectual stimulation afterward.

Children learn by testing hypotheses and evaluating feedback. Relevant feedback is any reaction that tells the child whether the hypothesis is justified or not. Children must comprehend what they are doing all the time they are learning. It is the possibility of making sense that stimulates them to learn. Many devices used in school to train the reader to note exact details in a text may result in producing a reader who, in making the effort to come more closely to grips with the exact meaning of an author, abandons the attempt to relate the significance of what he or she reads to his or her own social life. The teacher must, in helping children reveal their comprehension, be concerned with how and what children identify within their reading, what they feel to be synonymous and analogous to their own lives. We must provide opportunities for the reader to realise that other readers of the same text have found different ideas and understandings in it.

Literacy and Drama

The relationship between the two learning areas of drama and reading lies in the world of meaning. It is the idea of symbolisation and its role in the discovery and communication of meaning that connects drama and reading. Both areas are concerned with interaction. In story drama, the children enter into a dialogue, modifying and exploring symbols by changing and challenging each other's contributions. When reading, they enter into a dialogue with the author, with other readers and with themselves. Through discussion and analysis, they modify and develop their understanding of the author's meaning, as well as absorbing the diversity of meanings their classmates have taken from the text. In both cases, children are negotiating at the symbolic level.

Whether the situation the drama is based upon is original or from literature is of little significance. The drama must elaborate on facts to find hidden truths and universal concepts, not just retell events from memory. Weak drama, like weak reading, is concerned with words rather than with the meanings behind them.

Going beyond the text requires that the teacher's techniques somehow relate the concepts in the text to the child's experiences. In this way, fundamental memories brought forth by the intensity of the reading or drama experience, are tapped so that the resultant response is both personal and universal, and can be shared in the context of the literacy situation and the dramatic experience. The literacy code will be broken and the context made significant to the 'theory of the world' that each individual is in the process of creating while being educated – in the widest sense of the word.

How can drama assist children in building their own stories? How can we become co-constructors of the story with the children? In making meaning from text, children must go back and forth between the story they are reading or listening to, and the stories they know – their own personal narratives. They are in a very real sense building a personal story from the fiction alongside their own experiences, attempting to make sense of the story in order to make meaning in their lives. Until the child can make his or her story from the fictional one, there is no significant story for that child. The process of story continues beyond the end as the seed of another story readies itself for germination.

Drama is the act of crossing into the world of the story. In sharing drama, we agree to live as if the story we are enacting were true. We imagine the story, engage with it, struggle with its unfamiliar concepts, associate our own experiences with it and fill in its shape with our particular interpretation. We process the key events, images and themes of the story by living them out in drama. The process holds true whether the stimulus for the drama is a written story,

13

an oral tale or a group narration. Drama enables us to discover the heart of the story through its images. The voice of the group resonates off the voice of the text to create the voice of the drama.

Using the ideas of a story as cues for their own dramatic responses allows children to test the implications of what is written, and of their own responses to it. As teacher, I can draw upon the vast resources of the story as a way of stimulating and enriching the children's search for meaning in drama. Groups can test and clarify the implications of the text collectively, so that each person can see the difference in the various perceptions and interpretations, and can make decisions about his or her own responses.

In teaching children to read, we need to develop structures to help them work inside the printed form, as they experience the words. Similarly, teachers who are working with children in drama need to find ways of promoting learning as the drama is happening, not just afterwards, in presentation or in reflection time.

In drama, and in narrative, the context may be fictional but the emotional responses are real. Although the child is in a make-believe situation in story and drama, the real world continues to exist, and the learning for the child lies in the negotiation of meanings – symbolic and literal – taking place in both spheres. They re-examine the story's ideas, experimenting with them, learning to 'play' with the narrative and then, in reflection, coming to an understanding of both the story's possibilities and the art form used to create it.

Drama can help children see beyond literal meaning, even subconsciously, so that an understanding of the complexity and subtlety of meaning is applied to the story. The children pause in a fictional present, linger on an image, move forward, backwards and sideways, in an attempt to make meaning happen. Time can be altered, ideas juxtaposed. If story is being used as the source of a drama, then the child brings to the text an ability to hypothesise, to identify with and clarify what is happening in the story, in the drama and in his or her own life. The learning is integrated as he or she engages with the two art forms. When the child has translated a written symbol into experience, he or she can then re-examine the story in the light of this new experience. Drama lets us take a journey, as Tolkien says, 'there and back again'.

Making sense of a story demands that the children apply their own experiences to those in the story (Wells, 1986). As teachers, we need to constantly help the children go back and forth between the story and their own responses to it, translating the experiences of the story into the contexts of their own lives. Drama can help the children's own subjective world to come into play, increasing the meanings of the story as they live through the drama experience. If narrative and drama give form to thought and feeling, we can make use of one to build the other; we can use drama to clarify and strengthen the reading of story, and we can use the story to stimulate and enlighten the drama work. We can then engage children in the life blood of the story. For me, this must be the heart of our work in literacy.

Bibliography

Bolton, G., *New Perspectives on Classroom Drama*, Simon & Schuster, 1993.

Booth, D., *Guiding the Reading Process*, Pembroke Publishers, 1998.

Booth, D., *Story Drama*, Pembroke Publishers, 1994.

Wagner, B. J., *Building Moral Communities Through Educational Drama*, Ablex Publishing, 1999.

Wells, G., *The Meaning Makers*, Heinemann, 1986.

15

A Brighter Colour for the Literacy Hour

·using·

The Rainbow Fish by Marcus Pfister

Jo Boulton is a Senior Lecturer in the School of Education, University College, Northampton, where she is a specialist in English and Drama for the early years. Until last year she was a Curriculum Advisor with responsibility for Literacy Training in Northamptonshire.

The planning has been done. The big books have been bought, and after an incredibly short time the National Literacy Strategy has been introduced throughout the school. It is new, exciting and a completely different way of teaching and learning. It takes time to get used to the structure of the hour and the objectives, which are presented in the framework for teaching. However, it is going well. Much better than expected.

Yet, after only two terms of implementation, the Literacy Hour in its tightly structured and unrelenting format is in danger of becoming a repetitive and monotonous daily treadmill for the class teacher and her class of Year 1 children. Big book followed by worksheet was an easy and comfortable rut into which to fall. But the life and excitement of literacy teaching seems to be disappearing at the expense of pace, rigour and the demands of the term by term objectives. The cry is heard, 'Not another Big Book! Not another Literacy Hour!' Does it come from the teacher or the children? Nobody is quite sure.

The problem with any new educational initiative, however good, is that it must be able to change, grow and develop. If it is seen by teachers as an inflexible, rigid and static structure where there is no room at all for creativity and imagination, boredom and frustration can quickly set in. Flexibility, development and growth are essential for schools and teachers in order to maintain a vibrant and colourful curriculum. It is vital that teachers feel they can continue to use the many and varied teaching approaches that were successful before the literacy strategy imposed what many see as a 'straitjacket' on their teaching. After the suggested structures are in place in terms of planning and teaching, everyone involved knows what to expect, and things can start to evolve. Experimentation with different strategies and groupings can only strengthen the teacher's understanding of the processes involved in good quality literacy teaching.

I was asked to work with an experienced and concerned class teacher to demonstrate how drama could be easily integrated into the structure of the Literacy Hour. As part of a determined effort to ensure that the crucial aspects of creativity and imagination were kept in her literacy teaching, I was asked to show how drama could be used to support the teaching of the literacy objectives. I was asked also to show a variation of the teaching strategies she already used and to try and inject some colour and fun into the sessions.

The Project

This unit of work is designed to take place over five Literacy Hour sessions. The first four sessions follow the standard Literacy Hour structure, while the final hour is 'collapsed' to allow time for an extended drama session. This final session of the week is planned to consolidate and reinforce the work that has taken place in the previous four sessions but of course can be taught outside of the Literacy Hour if this is more appropriate. It can also be taught as a stand-alone drama lesson.

The Rainbow Fish project took place in a small rural primary school with a class of Year 1 children. The children had already had a great deal of imaginative play experience in a variety of pretend corner contexts set up by the class teacher and they had also some experience of whole class drama with the teacher taking on different roles. The class teacher had introduced the Literacy Hour in September and usually followed the suggested structure of the hour. The two main deviations from this were that she had decided to work with one guided group each day rather than two and children were reading on an individual basis outside the Literacy Hour. Guided reading was the one aspect of the strategy that the class teacher wanted to introduce when more resources were available and training had been completed.

In Year 1 Term 3 there is a significant emphasis on oral storytelling which includes retelling known stories, noticing the differences between spoken and written forms of stories and identifying the more formal features of story language. The text level work in this term consolidates and builds on the work that has taken place in the reception year and also the previous two terms of work in Year 1. The children have been given opportunities to compare 'told' versions with what the book 'says.' They have been involved in role-play to explore characters and re-enacted stories through role-play using dolls and puppets. This is, therefore, an ideal term to use drama within the Literacy

Hour as the objectives cry out for an active and interactive teaching approach to be used.

It was decided that the main focus of the drama work would be to teach and explore the text level objectives. Word and sentence level objectives were included where they would easily fit, but objectives were not included in the plans if they were not completely appropriate. As the focus was to be on text level work, I negotiated with the class teacher that the structure of the Literacy Hour would be reasonably flexible. There were no bells ringing after 15 minutes to make us move on to word level work, so we decided to be relaxed about the timings of the sessions which could be slightly different from day to day. However, the spirit of the Literacy Hour, with its demand for pace and direct teaching would be maintained.

A text was chosen that was appropriate for the suggested range to be studied in this term: 'Stories about fantasy worlds'. *The Rainbow Fish*, translated from the original Spanish by J. Alison James, was seen as an excellent stimulus for discussion of a range of issues as well as appropriate for teaching the chosen literacy learning objectives.

The Rainbow Fish is the most beautiful fish in the ocean, with wonderful silver scales. When Little Blue Fish asks for one, Rainbow Fish says, 'no'. He has no friends and seeks advice from the wise octopus who tells him that he would be happy if he gave up a scale. By the end of the story he has given all but one of his scales away, he has friends and is happy.

Learning Objectives

Word level

* to investigate and learn spellings of verbs with 'ed' and 'ing' endings
* new words from reading and shared experiences, and to make collections of personal interest or significant words and words linked to particular topics

Sentence level

* to read familiar texts aloud with pace and expression appropriate to the grammar, e.g. pausing at full stops, raising voice for questions
* to add question marks to questions

Text level

- to use phonological, contextual, grammatical and graphic knowledge to work out, predict and check the meanings of unfamiliar words and to make sense of what they read
- to notice the difference between spoken and written forms through retelling known stories: compare oral versions with written text
- to retell stories, to give the main points in sequence and to pick out significant incidents
- to prepare and retell stories orally, identifying and using some of the more formal features of story language
- to use titles, cover pages, pictures, and 'blurbs' to predict the content of unfamiliar stories
- to write about significant incidents from known stories

Assessment

There are a number of possibilities for assessment throughout this unit of work. It was decided to focus on assessing children's ability to retell stories giving the main points in sequence, their ability to prepare and retell stories orally using some formal features of story language, and also their willingness and ability to engage in the drama.

Lesson One

Whole Class Text Level Work (shared reading focusing on objectives T7 and T2)

I begin by talking to the class about the objectives we are going to cover this week. I tell them that we are focusing on retelling stories and that we will be using some drama to help us retell a story. I ask them to tell me about the story they had explored last week during their literacy sessions. Collectively, the children are able to tell me about the story in reasonable detail. They can remember the characters in the story and some of the things that happened, although the events are not related in chronological order. I ask what it is important to remember about a story when retelling it to someone else. I am told that you must get the story 'right' which they clarify for me as meaning 'not forgetting all the people and the things that happen and getting it in the right order'.

I ask the children about ways in which they had retold stories before. I give a few examples, as the children do not understand what I mean! When the penny drops, I am told that they have often acted out stories with their teacher narrating. Some of the class have re-enacted the story of *Goldilocks and the Three Bears* in an assembly. They have all taken part in the school nativity play at Christmas and retold the story of the birth of Jesus for the audience. Last term, some of them used puppets that they made to tell the story of the *Three Little Pigs* to the rest of the class. Some remember using extracts of dialogue from the text of a book that they had selected and highlighted to use in role-plays. They have obviously already had an enormous variety of experiences of telling and retelling stories.

I have prepared the cover of the big book version of *The Rainbow Fish* by covering the title. I ask the children to describe the fish. They tell me about the beautiful colours, the shiny scales and the smile on the lips of the fish. We read the blurb and talk about what that tells us about the story. We suggest some titles for the book – 'Beautiful Fish', 'Underwater Fish' and 'Fish has an Adventure' are some of the suggestions. We talk about the setting for the story. We talk about the colours used in the picture. What is it like under the sea? I reveal the title, which we read and admire. Of course, this is the perfect title! I tell the children that I am going to take on the role of the Rainbow Fish and they will be able to ask me some questions. We think about some of the things that they can ask Rainbow Fish. What do they want to know? They want to know if Rainbow Fish was a boy or a girl; how old it is; with whom it lives; what it likes to eat and other general questions like these. I cover the teacher's chair with a blue and silver cloth to make it a little more special and theatrical. I then go into role by walking over to the door and returning slowly to sit back down on the 'hot seat'.

After this hotseating session which lasts about five minutes, we talk about what we have learned about Rainbow Fish. I have been careful to give accurate information, but have also felt able to be creative with details that would not effect the story.

We then create a role on the wall for Rainbow Fish by drawing his outline on a piece of paper and adding single words and short phrases. The things that we know about Rainbow Fish from what he has said I write in red pen. Those things that we think or feel about him, I write in blue and other things that we were not sure about which we hope to find out later, I write in green. In red I write such words as, 'beautiful', 'shiny', 'lives in the sea', 'eats seaweed', 'lives alone', 'has no friends'. In blue I write, 'nice', 'sad', 'frightened', 'lonely' and 'shy'. In green I write, 'Why does he have shiny scales?' 'Where does he come from?'

We share the reading of the first four pages of text.

> A long way out in the deep blue sea there lived a fish. Not just an ordinary fish, but the most beautiful fish in the entire ocean. His scales were every shade of blue and green and purple, with sparkling silver scales among them.
>
> The other fish were amazed at his beauty. They called him Rainbow Fish. 'Come on, Rainbow Fish', they would call. 'Come and play with us!' But the Rainbow Fish would just glide past, proud and silent, letting his scales shimmer.
>
> One day, a little blue fish followed after him. 'Rainbow Fish,' he called, 'wait for me! Please give me one of your shiny scales. They are so wonderful, and you have so many.'
>
> 'You want me to give you one of my special scales? Who do you think you are? cried the Rainbow Fish. 'Get away from me!'
>
> Shocked, the Little Blue Fish swam away. He was so upset, he told all his friends what had happened. From then on, no one would have anything to do with the Rainbow Fish. They turned away when he swam by.

I have prepared the text with a few key words covered. I have covered the words 'shimmer', 'shiny', and 'upset'. During the reading, I discuss possible ways of predicting the covered words by using their contextual and grammatical knowledge. We talk about what we now know about the fish. What do we think about him? What do the other fish and sea creatures think of him?

Word level

We look back at the text we have read together and talk about any of the words we did not know. We then look to see whether we could add any of these words to the role on the wall. We add words such as 'sparkling silver scales', 'proud and silent', and 'shimmer'.

Group and independent work

The children work independently to develop a character for another fish or sea creature. We look at the pictures again and talk about the possibilities. They are asked not to choose Rainbow Fish, but create a completely new character that could possibly appear in the story. This will be important for the drama session on Friday when they will be asked to take on the role of the character they have developed today. The children draw a picture of the character and depending on their ability, write some words or sentences to describe it. The class teacher works with one group on the guided writing task.

Children who finish the activity are asked to write words and phrases from the role on the wall for Rainbow Fish on to previously prepared paper scale shapes. These are added to a classroom display about the story that is created during the week with work completed in art sessions.

Plenary

I tell the children that I will be in role as a character called Shining Fish. I show them a picture I have drawn and read a few sentences I have written describing 'myself.' I ask each of them to introduce themselves as the character they have created.

Lesson Two

Whole Class Text Level Work (shared reading focusing on objectives T2 and S7)

In this lesson, there is no clear distinction between the text level and word level work in the first 30 minutes. Objectives are addressed as they occur.

I start this session by recapping on the story so far. We retell the story in as much detail as we can and I record the main events on a large piece of paper that is set out in the form of a simple storyboard. We start with the title.

1. The Rainbow Fish.	**2.** Rainbow Fish lives in the sea. He has beautiful scales.	**3.** Little Blue Fish asks for a scale. Rainbow Fish says 'No!'	**4.** All of the other fish swim away from Rainbow Fish Not his friends.

We read the next page which tells of Rainbow Fish's loneliness. The starfish couldn't help, but suggested that he should speak to the wise octopus. I have covered the word 'loneliest' and the children predict words like 'saddest', 'angry', and 'mean'. I encourage them to read the sentence aloud inserting the suggested words to find out which one sounds best. Perhaps the wise octopus might be able to help Rainbow Fish to decide whether to give away one of his shiny scales to the Little Blue Fish. We consider what might be said in the conversation between Rainbow Fish and Octopus. What questions will Rainbow Fish ask? What questions will Octopus ask? Two or three possible questions are framed and written on the flip chart, emphasising the use of the question mark by using a coloured pen.

The questions are read aloud and we talk about the way our voices go up and down when we ask questions. We practice asking the questions in different ways. We talk about possible answers to the questions. What could Octopus answer? I explain that they are going to work in pairs for the next activity. One of the pair will be Rainbow Fish and the other will be Octopus. They will be able to practice asking the questions and giving answers and they are encouraged to be creative and use their own ideas.

The children then work in pairs. One of them asks the question and the other answers it. It does not go smoothly at first. Some pairs are not completely sure what to do. So I demonstrate with a partner. After this things improve and the Rainbow Fishes and Octopuses have some good conversations. I ask for some volunteer pairs to show us the conversation that they think might have taken place. Nearly everyone wants to show the work that has been done! We only have time to see a couple now but we are able to see more at the end of the afternoon during story-time.

> 'I have been waiting for you,' said Octopus with a deep voice. 'The waves have told me your story. This is my advice. Give a glittering scale to each of the other fish. You will no longer be the most beautiful fish in the sea, but you will discover how to be happy.'

We talk about the advice that Rainbow Fish has been given. Do we think this is good advice?

Guided and independent work

The children work independently to fill in the questions that Rainbow Fish asked Octopus in speech bubbles. Some children use prepared sheets while the most able children are asked to draw their own bubbles and are asked to write at least five questions. The focus here is the correct use of question marks and the children are reminded how to write them. See the diagram on page 24.

Plenary

During the plenary session I take on the role of Octopus. I prepare the group for the activity by explaining that they will all be in role as Rainbow Fish and will in turn be able to ask one of the questions that they have written down. As Octopus, I will answer the questions. We decide who will ask the first question and how we will know who comes next. They decide it is best to sit in a circle. They all sit on the floor in the book corner. I walk over to the door and I put on a brown cloak. I walk slowly back and sit down on a chair.

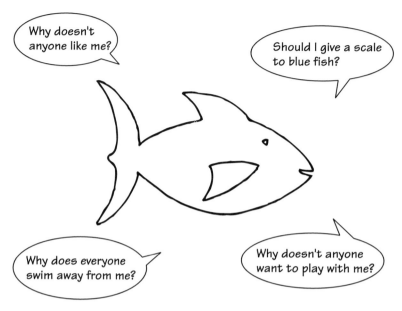

Why doesn't anyone like me?

Should I give a scale to blue fish?

Why does everyone swim away from me?

Why doesn't anyone want to play with me?

24

Diagram for guided and independent work

You have come to ask my advice Rainbow Fish. What can I do to help you with your problem?

This goes really well. I feel pleased that everyone has a question to ask and there is quite a variety. Clearly there is some repetition, but I take each question as if it is heard for the first time and I make sure I give variations on the same answer. I feel pleased that they have covered a great deal in this session.

Lesson Three

Whole Class Text Level Work (shared reading focusing on objectives T5 and T6)

We sit in a circle. I start the session by going back to the storyboard and we read what is there. We then fill in another section, marking Rainbow Fish's visit to Octopus. I tell the class that today we will be thinking about the ways in which the same story can be told differently by different people. I use an example of a playground incident where someone was pushed over, when there were two very different versions of the same event. We talk about different points of view. I ask the class to tell me who is telling the story in the text of *The Rainbow Fish* as we read it. This is quite a confusing concept and I have to ask various questions such as 'Is the Rainbow Fish telling us the story?'and 'How do we know that octopus is not telling the story?' I introduce the idea of the narrator and we try to think of any other books that they have had which uses a narrator.

I then tell them that it is important to use the right kind of language when we are telling stories. We talk about what this means. Michael says he thinks it means that you have to sound like a book when you tell a story and make sure you don't swear! Storm says that stories all start with 'Once upon a time . . .'. We think about whether this is true or not. We decide that it is important to choose good words so that it will be interesting to listen to, as there are no pictures to look at.

We remind ourselves of Octopus' words: 'The waves have told me your story'. I ask them to think about what the waves have told Octopus. We have a look at the storyboard that we started yesterday. I remind them that during the plenary session yesterday they were all in role as Rainbow Fish. Today they are all going to be the waves telling the story of what has happened to Octopus. We discuss the fact that the waves are rather like narrators but they may have strong feelings about one or other of the characters and this will be shown by the way in which they tell the story – the words they use and also the tone of voice. I tell them that today I am going to be Octopus again and that they must try and put lots of details in to the story to make it last longer than two minutes. They are also reminded that when this part comes in the story, the Rainbow Fish has not yet gone to have a chat to Octopus so they cannot use that part of the story to tell.

We discuss a good opening for the story that the waves will tell. Madeleine suggests we start with wave sounds and then something like, 'Octopus, we want to tell you about something that has happened'. I ask for a volunteer to start. We decide that I will nod when the next 'wave' is to carry on. I respond to each wave as they add to the story. Not surprisingly, the story doesn't last for very long. About five 'waves' have spoken. I decide that we can have another quick go with a few more 'waves.' This time I ask for five volunteers to sit in the middle of the circle and repeat the storytelling process. This goes well.

I then ask the class to think how the story might change if the Little Blue Fish was telling it. Would he see things differently? What tone of voice would he use? The class decided that Little Blue Fish would try to get Octopus' sympathy and that he might use a quiet whining tone. We suggested ways in which the story could start and then I asked for volunteers to be Little Blue Fish. I chose from those who had not yet had a turn. The change in tone was very noticeable. The group uses a very babyish register and a moaning tone.

'There's a new fish in our part of the ocean.'
'It's not fair Octopus, I don't like that new fish.'
'He's mean.'
'He won't give me a scale.'

Word level work

There is only about seven minutes of time left as I have been carried away by our enthusiasm for the storytelling. I tell them that we are on a search for words that have 'ing' endings. We look at the text and I make a list on the flip chart. I write words such as 'waiting', 'glittering', 'dazzling', 'shimmering'. I ask them what kind of words they are picking out. We identify the words as verbs. They have explored verbs in detail over the previous few weeks. We talk about how to change the verbs in to the past tense. I give examples from the text and change the tense of the verb from present to past by changing the ending from 'ing' to 'ed'.

Guided and independent work

The children work individually to make their own zigzag storybook of the Rainbow Fish. I demonstrate how to fold the A3 paper. There are 8 pages to fill and today we design the cover and write or draw the first three events from the story. These are already recorded on the class storyboard so in effect the children are simply making their own version. Some draw pictures, some write a word or caption while others are able to write in more detail. I am pleased at their enthusiasm for making the books and decide that we may need to find some extra time to finish them.

Plenary

We look at some of the books and discuss the importance of the front and back covers.

Lesson Four

Whole class text level work (shared reading focusing on objectives T3 and W8)

We sit in the circle again today. I start by asking the class what they think might happen next in the story. We read the next two pages which tell of Rainbow Fish's distress at Octopus's suggestion. He couldn't bear the thought of giving away his scales. But Little Blue Fish asks again, saying he doesn't want to upset Rainbow Fish. He just wants one little scale. Rainbow Fish wonders if he wouldn't miss just one.

I ask the class how they think Rainbow Fish might be feeling at this moment in the story. Some give straightforward and simple responses such as 'He's sad' while others give more reflective statements such as 'He's feeling very confused about what to do about it', or 'I think he's unhappy because he can't decide what he should do'.

I tell the children that we are going to think more about Rainbow Fish's thoughts and feelings at this moment in the story. I ask the children who have already given some ideas, to rephrase the thought as if Rainbow Fish himself was saying it. So instead of 'He's sad', Gemma said, 'I'm sad'. I asked the group to think of a thought that Rainbow Fish could be thinking and tell it to the person next to them. I felt that this would give confidence to the more insecure members of the class. I spotted those who had no ideas of their own and quickly intervened to help them. I made it clear that it didn't matter if two people spoke the same thoughts because thoughts often tumble around in our minds when we are thinking about something important.

I stood in the middle of the circle and the class stood around me. I told them that I was going to be Rainbow Fish and that they were going to speak my thoughts when I touched them on the shoulder. I walked around the circle as if I was swimming and walked in between the children. I stood behind individuals and they spoke my thoughts.

It was not perfect, but it went well with most children saying something. I felt that this was quite a difficult task to ask of Year 1 children but we were all pleased with the result. If there had been time I would have liked to have repeated the activity and this time perhaps I would have asked the children to walk up to Rainbow Fish who would have been sitting or standing in the middle of the circle. They could then have spoken his thoughts as they touched him on the shoulder. Rainbow Fish would have responded through facial expression or gesture to the different thoughts. This would have been a good talking point and we could have discussed the two different drama structures.

We read on to discover that Rainbow Fish gives a scale to Little Blue Fish. I covered the word 'peculiar' in the sentence after he has given away his first scale: 'A rather *peculiar* feeling came over the Rainbow Fish'. We spend a while predicting what it could be. I reveal the word and we discuss what we think it means. The end is read so the children discover that Rainbow Fish decides to give up his beautiful shiny scales to the other fish and they accept him as a friend.

For me, the moral here is questionable and it was fascinating to listen to the children's responses and ideas. Most of them agreed that it was only right that Rainbow Fish gave up his scales so that the other fish would be his friends. They said that he was selfish and shouldn't keep them all for himself as that showed how greedy he was. I tried to draw parallels with playground situations where sweets were perhaps the issue but the children were very clearly of the opinion that sharing was the fair thing to do. If that meant bullying in the process then that seemed to be acceptable. I asked the children to think of any other books that they knew with a similar moral or theme. They suggested titles such as 'Greedy Zebra' and we discussed the similarities and differences in the two stories.

To finish this session we noted down the main points of the story on the class storyboard.

5. He visits Octopus for advice.	**6.** He gives one scale to Little Blue Fish.	**7.** He gave one scale to each fish.	**8.** They were his friends.

Word level

We looked back through the text and chose some words that the children thought were interesting either because they hadn't heard them before or because they sounded good! We chose words such as 'whiz', 'glimmer' and 'glitter'. We added these to the class dictionary after making sure we all knew what they meant.

Guided and independent work

The children continue to work individually on their zigzag books. They use the class storyboard as a prompt, but I encourage them to use their own ideas and expand on the notes we have made as a class. Two of the more able children had completed their work quickly and had started work on a picture of Rainbow Fish using a paint package on the computer.

Plenary

Not all the books are complete and will be finished later. We share some of those that are finished. They look really good. We talk about alternative endings to the story. What else could have happened? One child suggests that Rainbow Fish could leave the area and find some new friends. Another suggests that he could be chased away by the fish. Another says that a shark eats him! Michael says he gets flushed down a toilet. There is always one! I take it all very seriously!

I tell the class that tomorrow we are going to spend the whole of the Literacy Hour telling the story of Rainbow Fish using drama. We will not be using the book this time. We will all take on roles in the story and we will see if our story is exactly the same as the one in the book or perhaps it will be different!

Lesson Five

Whole class drama (T5)

This session concentrates on retelling the story, giving the main points in order and picking out significant incidents. The classroom is arranged for drama and the children start the session sitting in a circle on the floor.

Introduction

I tell the group that I will start the drama by telling the opening of the story as a narrator. I will be asking individuals to add details and ideas to the story as it goes along. They will know when to speak because I will look directly at them. I will be using formal story language and will expect them to use it too.

Narration and storytelling

A long way out in the deep ocean where the water is sparkling and clear, the fish and other sea creatures play all day among the weeds. There are all kinds of beautifully coloured fish. Some are red and some are . . . [child provides detail] Others are . . . and some are . . . The fish play with the other sea creatures such as Octopus and the . . . and the . . . They play all kinds of games together such as hide and seek and . . . and . . . They all live very happily together in their beautiful undersea world. The fish and the sea creatures like it in their part of the ocean because it is beautiful and . . . and . . . Everyone is happy there.

Developing a role

I ask the group to sit in pairs. I ask them all to think about the fish or the sea creature they created on Monday. I ask each one of them to pretend that they are that creature and talk to their partner in role. I give an example: 'Hello, my name is Shining Fish. I am green and yellow and I like eating weeds'. They have a go at talking in pairs.

Enactment

I tell the group that in the next part of the story the classroom will be the ocean and we will all be the fish and sea creatures living there. I ask them to stand or sit in a space of their own and I indicate that when I clap my hands they will be the fish and the creatures in the story and can move around the space. Shining Fish will be chatting with them and asking questions about what they are doing. I tell them that when I clap again they must freeze. They are used to this stop signal. I narrate that it is a lovely bright morning. All the creatures are going about their business, playing or chatting with each other in the ocean. I clap my hands and the action starts. This is clearly the best part of the whole session for the children. They swim, crawl, wriggle and lurch around the room. In role as Shining Fish, I go up to individuals and ask who they are and what they are doing today.

Still image and thought tap

After a few minutes, I clap again and the action freezes. I go up to some to whom I have not already spoken and ask them what they think about living in the ocean, who they think are their best friends, and so on. I restart the action again with a clap and repeat this two or three times until I have spoken to most of the group. A possible problem here could be that someone mentions Rainbow Fish. The teacher in role as Shining Fish should accept what is said but emphasise that she has not heard or seen anything of this new fish yet.

Meeting

I tell the group that in the next part of the story they are going to be called to a meeting by Shining Fish. There is something important to tell them all and to talk about. I ask them to decide where they will be in the ocean. Will they stand or sit? We arrange the space. I am in role as Shining Fish. I welcome them all to the meeting. I ask if they are all well and I ask a few what they have been doing. I say that I have heard rumours about a new fish that has come to this part of the ocean. Has any one heard anything about him or seen him? I ask what he looks like and they describe him to me. Leo, (Stripey Fish) tells me that the new fish is called Rainbow Fish. Ellie, (Shark) says he isn't friendly. Rosie, (Crab) says he has shiny scales and won't give any to her. I say that I have heard that Little Blue Fish has asked for a scale too. I ask why they want the scales. They say they are shiny and that they want one because they are pretty. I ask whether any of them have tried to make friends or if they have spoken to Rainbow Fish. Grace, (Seahorse) says she thinks he is shy. Oliver, (Green Fish) thinks he'd like to talk to Rainbow Fish.

Circle of thoughts

I explain that all of the creatures are going to have the chance to tell Rainbow Fish how they feel about him. I say that some of the creatures may want to be friends or some may be angry with him. I place a shiny cloak on a chair in the centre of the circle to represent Rainbow Fish. In turn, the sea creatures go up to the chair and say how they feel about Rainbow Fish. I start by giving an example in role as Shining Fish. There is a good mixture. Not all of them want a scale. Some think that they'd like to play with him.

Mind Voices

I ask the group what happens next in the story. They tell me that Starfish advises Rainbow Fish to go and talk to the wise Octopus. I remind them of the work that we have already done on Tuesday when I was in role as Octopus and they asked me questions. I ask if they can remember the sort of things that Octopus said to Rainbow Fish. We remember that he said, 'Give up your scale, it will make you happy'. I ask them all to whisper the phrase 'It will make you happy'. We practice whispering the phrase getting louder and louder until we are shouting. I explain what will happen now. I walk in to the circle and put on the Rainbow Fish cloak. I sit in the middle of the circle. I say that I can hear the voice of Octopus in my head telling me to give up my scale because it will make me happy. They start to whisper and then on a signal from me begin to get louder and louder. I end the scene by shouting stop and holding my head in my hands saying, 'How could I ever be happy without them?'

Enactment and teacher in role

In the final part of the drama, the sea creatures are again going about their business and the teacher in role as Rainbow Fish arrives asking to speak to them all. He tells them that he has decided to give them a present of one of his scales, but not because they are asking for one. He realises that he has more than he needs and knows that he will be beautiful inside even if he is no longer quite so beautiful on the outside.

Ritual

Rainbow Fish asks the creatures to line up and come forward one at a time. He gives each of them a scale in a ritualistic way and tells them to take care of the scale, as it is special. He invites them all to his cave and hopes that they will all become good friends.

Reflection in role

I want the group to have the opportunity to think about the actions of Rainbow Fish in this version of the story. I tell them that I am going to return as Shining Fish. I dress in the cloak and run puffing into the group, apologising for not having been there. I am amazed to see them all with scales and want to know how they had got them. I hoped that they hadn't stolen them from Rainbow Fish or bullied him in to giving them away. They explain what had happened. I probe further to ask how they feel. Some say they are pleased others said they feel sorry that they have been unkind. There is a much greater range of responses about the moral of the story than during the discussion yesterday.

Discussion

The session ends with a short discussion about the differences between our story and the original text. We go back to the objectives that I introduced to the group on Monday and we think about how we have covered them through our work.

The literacy work had been varied and active. The class teacher and I discussed how the drama methods could be used with other texts in the following weeks. She particularly noted that the children showed enormous confidence during the final session. She felt this had been built up during the previous lessons when shorter drama activities had been used during the Literacy Hours.

Final thoughts

Despite my initial fears that drama would be marginalised and possibly completely neglected in the primary school with the rigidity of the Literacy Hour I am excited about the future. There is a definite place for drama structures to be used within the Literacy Hour itself to shape and explore issues within different types of text. The versatility of these drama structures enables teachers to provide active and interactive opportunities for young children to search for meanings and truths that may seem beyond their existing schema. New thoughts, new ways of looking and seeing, new voices, visions and colours are there to be found and tried out in drama time. Using drama to excite and inspire children, enabling them to reach for fresh feelings and meanings is really possible within the Literacy Hour and essential as part of every child's entitlement.

Lesson Guide

Resources Two different pieces of shiny material for Rainbow Fish and Shining Fish, one piece of dull material for Octopus, flip chart or large paper and pens, big book version of *The Rainbow Fish*.

33

Time Four Literacy Hour sessions and one hour for drama.

Lesson One

* **Prediction:** Predict title.
* **Hot seat:** The fish in the picture.
* **Role on the wall:** Things we know about, things we feel about and things we want to find out about the fish.
* **Read:** The first four pages of text, predicting concealed words.
* **Word collection:** Of unknown and new words.
* **Create a character:** Pupils draw and write details about a new character.
* **Teacher in role:** As Shining Fish. Sea creatures introduce themselves.

Year 1 • Term 3
T2, 7
W8

Lesson Two

* **Storyboarding:** The story so far.
* **Read:** Page 5 of the text.
* **Framing questions:** To ask Octopus.
* **Pairs:** Rainbow Fish asking Octopus the framed questions.
* **Performance:** Of pair work to the whole class.
* **Read:** Pages 7 & 8.
* **Speech bubbles:** The questions that Rainbow Fish asked Octopus.
* **Teacher in role:** As Octopus answering the written questions.

Year 1 • Term 3
T2, 13
S7

Lesson Three

Year 1 • Term 3
T2, 13
S7

- **Storyboarding:** Further incidents in the story.
- **Discussion:** Storytelling from different perspectives. Formal language.
- **Read:** Page 7 again.
- **Storytelling:** In role as the waves.
- **Storytelling:** In role as the Little Blue Fish.
- **Word search:** 'ing' endings.
- **Bookmaking:** Individual zigzag books of the story.
- **Sharing:** Individual books. Discussion of covers.

Lesson Four

Year 1 • Term 3
T3
W8

- **Read:** Pages 8 & 9.
- **Predict:** Thoughts and feelings of Rainbow Fish.
- **Speaking thoughts:** Of Rainbow Fish.
- **Read:** To the end.
- **Discussion:** About moral of the story.
- **Storyboarding:** The final incidents in the story.
- **Word collection:** New and interesting words to add to class dictionary.
- **Bookmaking:** Continue with individual zigzag books.
- **Discussion:** Alternative endings to the story.

Lesson Five

Year 1 • Term 3
T5

- **Narration and storytelling:** Scene setting through interactive storytelling.
- **Developing a role:** In role as sea creatures created previously. Introductions and chatting in pairs.
- **Enactment:** Under the sea. Everyday life of the sea creatures. Teacher in role.
- **Still image and thought tap:** What do the creatures think about their part of the ocean?
- **Meeting:** Define the space. Teacher in role introduces problem of new fish to the area.
- **Circle of thoughts:** Questions the sea creatures want to ask Rainbow Fish.
- **Mind voices:** Collective chanting of phrase. Teacher in role responding.
- **Enactment and teacher in role:** Rainbow Fish tells the sea creatures he will give them each a scale.
- **Ritual:** Rainbow Fish gives a scale to each creature.
- **Reflection:** Teacher in role as Shining Fish asks the creatures to explain what has happened.
- **Discussion:** Similarities and differences between drama and written text.

Calling Across The Sea

≈using≈

When My Ship Comes In by Alan Gibbons and illustrated by Joe Rice

Paul Bunyan is an advisory teacher for Drama, and the Head of the Expressive Arts Advisory Team for Northamptonshire. He is currently Chair of the Drama Standing Committee for the National Association for the Teaching of English.

Part of my work is concerned with support for newly qualified teachers. One such teacher and I agreed to use *When My Ship Comes In* (printed in big book format) to explore the relationship between Drama and the Literacy Strategy. The activities described here were used with children in Years 2 and 3. My focus was the statement on page 1 of the National Literacy Strategy which claims:

> Literacy unites the important skills of reading and writing. It also involves speaking and listening which, although they are separately identified in the [National Literacy] framework, are an essential part of it. Good oral work enhances pupils' understanding of language in both oral and written forms and of the way language can be used to communicate. It is also an important part of the process through which pupils read and compose texts.
>
> *(Department for Education, 1998)*

The Project

The text *When My Ship Comes In* is set in *the big city of Liverpool* in 1901. It focuses on two boys, the un-named narrator, the son of an African immigrant and a Liverpudlian woman, and his friend, Eddie. The boys are poor and have to make do with boots that they have outgrown and which are full of holes. The narrator misses his father, a seaman, who spends long periods away at sea. As they play and dream around the streets and docks, the narrator is unaware that his father has returned home after a long voyage with a present for the boy: a new pair of boots.

Learning Objectives

* To provide the children with a range of contexts which make demands on their capacity to talk and listen.

* To create fictional contexts in which children can write in appropriate registers.
* To give children lively environments in which they can read purposefully and accurately.

Word level

* To teach pupils new words from reading linked to particular topics, to build individual collections of personal interest or significant words.
* To give pupils the opportunity to use synonyms and other alternative words and phrases that express the same or similar meanings.

Sentence level

* To give pupils the opportunity to read texts aloud with pace and expression appropriate to the grammar and to re-read own writing for sense and punctuation.
* To enable pupils to investigate and recognise a range of other ways of presenting texts.

Text level

* To help pupils to identify and discuss characters, e.g. appearance, behaviour, qualities and to discuss how they are described in the text.
* To enable pupils to become aware of character and dialogue, e.g. by role playing parts.
* To prepare and retell stories individually or through role-play in groups using dialogue and narrative.

Assessment

This project provides many opportunities for drama to stimulate written work and then for this to be used back in the drama. This writing can be assessed according to the word and sentence level criteria in the Literacy Strategy. There are also many opportunities to assess speaking and listening skills.

Below are a few very simple dramatic conventions which I used with this text. Most of them can be used with other texts just as easily.

Activities

Teacher in Role Presentation

In order to stimulate interest in the characters and themes of the text, I had prepared a role for the children to observe. The children sat in a circle. In the centre of their circle I placed a pair of children's lace-up boots similar to the ones illustrated on the back cover of the book. The boots had a price tag attached to them. I asked the children to look at them carefully and describe what they could see. The children offered detailed observations using vocabulary such as 'toe', 'heel', 'laces', 'sole' and 'leather'. I explained to the children that I was going to pretend to be someone else who is also looking at the boots. I asked them to listen and watch carefully to find out what they could about the character from the story they were about to encounter. I often find it helpful to use background music or sound effects. Here I used sound effects of the sea.

Picking up a prepared cloth bundle, I swung it over my shoulder and entered the circle in role as the sailor (the boy's father). I stopped to look at the boots. While looking at them, in role as the boy's father, I spoke, as if thinking out loud:

> If only I could afford to buy such a pair of boots as a present. I've been at sea so long. I'd heard they crafted fine leather work in this port. If I keep working hard on the ship I shall save enough money to buy them.

After one more wistful look, I walked out of the circle, putting down the bundle and fading the soundtrack, thereby indicating to the children that I was out of role and the drama had stopped.

The children discussed what they thought about the character they had met. We looked at the picture in the book of the father by a ship with his bundle. Children's suggestions about him from the teacher role and from the picture were written on Post-its. They stuck their Post-its onto the page. Their suggestions included:

> He's a sailor
> He hasn't got much money
> He likes to buy presents
> He's been away from home for a long time.

Shared reading

The children looked at the back cover of the book. There is a picture of a pair of boots. We read out the blurb:

> Somewhere in the big city of Liverpool, nearly a hundred years ago, a little

boy longs for a pair of new boots. Read this book to find out how, one wonderful day, the boy gets his wish.

I then asked the children if they had heard the proverbial phrase 'when my
ship comes in'. I asked when this phrase might be used. We also investigated
other individual phrases such as why the writer uses the words 'longs for' and
what might be another way of saying them. When the children looked at the
front cover picture, they guessed at the historical context, the characters and
the activity.

Script writing

The children involved were familiar with models of play texts and had spent
some time identifying what distinguishes a play text from prose containing
dialogue. I read the following extract:

> I see Eddie playing in the court between my front door and his.
> 'The sun's cracking the flags today,' shouts Eddie. It isn't, but I know what
> he means. Eddie's my best mate. His boots don't have holes in them, but
> they're a size too small now and they hurt. But he has no money for new
> ones either.
> 'Do you want to go for a walk?' he asks.
> 'Where?'
> 'Let's go into town,' says Eddie. We set off together, but I don't want to walk.
> I want to run. My boots flap around and my feet begin to hurt. I stop to let
> Eddie catch up, and we stare across the Mersey together.

The children identified the speech marks in the text. They then used a play text
writing frame which enabled them to write the name of the character who is
speaking ('Boy' or 'Eddie') on the left-hand side of the page and the words the
characters spoke on the right, as in a formal script. More able pupils were
given a play text writing frame which included a space for stage directions. A
more able group still, improvised an extended dialogue between the two
friends and converted this into script. Some of the children used audio
equipment to record their scripts.

Freeze frame text activity

This is an interesting and challenging activity that can be used with other pictures from other story books. Using a picture from page 3, we sculpted two
volunteers into the exact positions occupied by the boy's mother and father in

the picture. While the children held their positions in the picture, I took a plain piece of paper and held it on the wall behind them. I asked the group what they thought it was and what they thought might be written on it. Answers ranged from 'posters' to 'advertisements'. I then held it above the door. It was seen as a 'shop name' or a 'closed sign'. I then folded the paper and put it into the hand of the child in the Mother's position. I asked the group what the paper might now represent and what they imagined was written on it. 'A shopping list', 'a letter?'. Extending the idea further I took the same piece of paper and folded it again and put it in an envelope and put it in the hand of the child sculpted as the Father. What is the paper now? The children offered their ideas – 'A letter from the shipping company', 'A bill which has to be paid'.

I finally screwed the paper into a ball and placed it on the floor at the feet of the couple asking, 'What might the paper represent now?'

Next the children constructed their own 'text props' to be placed in the picture, and discussed where it should be placed. The children worked in pairs creating two copies of their text. One copy was to be placed in the sculpted picture. They held on to the other. When all the pairs were ready, we recreated our still image. The pairs, one at a time, carefully placed their text in the appropriate place in the image. On the count of three the children in the picture came to life and responded to the text props according to where they had been placed. For one pair they would have to point up at a wall, for another take the paper out of a pocket. As each piece of paper was revealed, the pair who made it, read out the copy of the text they had retained as if the characters in the drama were reading the texts in their heads or to each other. When the reading started the actors froze once again to form a second still image.

Pictures and guided walks

Again, this activity is easily transferred to other location pictures in other texts. We looked at the double page picture of Liverpool on pages 12 & 13. I asked them to identify all the details they could see. They pointed out the steam trains, the factory, the clock, the horse and cart and the bridge. I encouraged them to take the opportunity to emphasise some of the technical language, such as 'viaduct' and 'winch'.

The following activity grew out of the children's familiarity with these pages and required a degree of concentrated speaking and listening. They worked in pairs, A and B. A was asked to imagine living in this city, and knowing it very well. B was to pretend to be a visitor, new to the place. I held the pages up so that all could see. As were asked to lead Bs around some of the places shown in the picture, while As kept their eyes open and Bs' eyes remained shut. The children were used to working actively and responsibly in pairs, so As led Bs slowly around the room, giving a spoken commentary as they went, pointing out imagined details, including sights, sounds and smells. Where a class is not able to work in this way, they could sit in pairs with the As tracing their fingers around an imaginary map explaining to Bs what they could 'see'. Finally, the Bs told the class what they had seen, smelt, or heard on their guided tour. I intervened with questions to make demands on the children's descriptive, functional or technical language:

> Describe what it was like in the tunnel.
> How did the man get the load from the cart into the building?

The children wanted to have another go at this. A development may be for the children to write a simple guide to this dockland area perhaps modelled on the language and style of a guide from an industrial museum or local town guide pamphlet.

Still image and soundtrack

There is a picture in the book depicting the narrator and his friend, Eddie, staring out to sea. We wondered what the boys could see. There were suggestions about the work that was going on and the fact that it was a quayside. One of the children referred to the boys as 'our two friends from the story'. Two volunteers took the roles of the two friends. I asked the other children from the class to come up one at a time and sculpt the two pupils until they represented the characters in the picture exactly. When this was done I asked the class to look at the sculpted picture for a while and imagine what the boys were thinking as they looked out over the sea. I introduced a soundtrack at this point. I used a sound effects tape of the sea, but other sea music would do, too. It served to convey the atmosphere, frame the drama and help the children in role, and the rest of the class, to concentrate. I asked the children to make the characters' private thoughts public. From where they were sitting, one by one, the children spoke the thoughts. (The children could have stepped forward to place a hand on the character whose thoughts they voiced.)

> I wish I could go to sea.
> I think I can see a boat.
> My dad's out there somewhere.

Messages across the sea in a corporate voice

I read the next piece of text.

> I squint against the sunlight and look at the sparkling waters. My dad's out there on the ocean where the world smells of salt and the floor rolls when he walks.

I wanted the children to create words across the sea; to imagine what the son and the father would say to each other over the waves, if only they could. I called upon the child who took the role of the boy at the railings earlier to take up his position again. Another child took the role of the father and was sculpted like the Father seen struggling against the elements at sea in the picture. We used a rope and a sowester as props. We discussed what the father and son might say to each other. A group of volunteers stood in an arc behind each character. Each group created the voice of their character between them, adding to and supporting or enriching what was said before. The voices were heard calling over the sea from the son to the father and the father to the son. The use of a taped soundtrack was useful here, too. This time it was of an angry sea. Again, the soundtrack signalled the beginning and the end of the dramatic activity. This activity supports shy children because they do not have to take on the full responsibility for the dialogue. The children adjusted their voices, finding the register appropriate to the desperate situation and bearing in mind the relationship between the two characters.

Dialogue pairwork

At the end of the book there is a picture of the boy and his mother looking at a brand new pair of boots on a table in their home. The children wrote a dialogue for the mother and son which would explain how the boots came to be there.

Bibliography

DfEE, *National Literacy Strategy*: 'What is Literacy?', p3, The Stationery Office, 1998.

Gibbons, A. & Rice, J., *When My Ship Comes In*, Collins Pathways, 1996.

41

Lesson Guide

Resources A classroom space, an overhead projector and screen or plain wall, Post-its, felt tip pens, paper and pencils, a pair of lace up boots, preferably children's size, a bundle in a cloth or sack. Optional: an audio tape/CD recorder, sound effects tape of the sea, sea shanties or other sea music.

Time The literacy work could take two or more Literacy Hour sessions to complete if you are to develop the children's skills, and circulate, guiding the group tasks. You may wish to integrate the following approaches to the text into the Literacy Hour framework or to use extended whole English time to develop the children's language; not only to meet the requirements of the Literacy Strategy but also in relation to the Speaking and Listening requirements of the reviewed National English Curriculum.

Activities

Year 2 • Year 3 **Term 2**	● **Word collection:** Boots placed in centre. Children describe the character and interpret possible circumstances.
T6 **T3**	● **Teacher in role:** As boy's father. Wants to buy boots as a present for his son.
	● **Interpretation:** Children discuss character of the father.
W10 • W17	● **Shared reading:** Class collectively read and discuss back cover blurb.
Term 2 • Term 1 **S6** **T5** **Term 3** **S4**	● **Script writing:** Read extract. Children translate words within speech marks into play text format and then write their own script using accepted terminology.
T14 T20	● **Freeze frame text activity:** Still imaging task. Placing text in picture.
W10 • W17	● **Guided walks:** Using double page picture, children identify all details. In pairs, they are to describe a walk around Liverpool.
T4, 5, 6 Term 1 **T3**	● **Still imaging (with soundtrack):** Two children are 'sculpted' to represent the two boys looking out to sea. Others speak out loud the boys' hopes and fears.
T3	● **Corporate voice:** Use picture and texts from pages 10 & 11. Children together construct the conversation that the father and son would have if they were able to.
Term 1 • Term 2 **T10** **T7** **T3,4**	● **Dialogue pair work:** Children write dialogue for mother and son, discussing how new boots came to be at home.

Giant Steps in Writing

·using·

Giant by Juliet and Charles Snape

Sue Boshell is in her final year of a primary teacher training course at University College, Northampton. The primary school where she carried out this project has appointed her to its staff for September.

I am a mature student in my final year of a four-year teacher training course. The English Specialist programme includes a course in drama which inspired me so much that my dissertation was an exploration into the effectiveness of using drama as a teaching tool in the writing strand of the National Literacy Strategy. It is this which forms the basis of this chapter.

One of the things that I noticed during my school placements is the reluctance of teachers to use drama as a teaching technique. Kitson and Spiby (1997) suggest that this may be because of confusion about what drama actually is and the array of types of drama. It may also be that some teachers are concerned about the informality of the subject and that they may lose control of the situation. However, I have used several drama techniques and found that both myself and the pupils have not only enjoyed, but benefited from the experience.

The use of role-play engages children in their work on a very personal level and it is this that can enrich their writing. The feelings and thoughts of the character played by the pupil influences the written response of the pupil when writing from 'remembered role' (Booth, 1998). The impact of being both participant in the drama and yet also a spectator invokes a highly potent and evocative response. The role still has a forcible degree of influence over the writer. It matters to the children what they write because there is a real purpose to write. They are writing from first-hand experience about the events that have had an effect on them. They write to those who determine the events in their dramatic fictional worlds. An understanding and awareness of audience is generated through the selection of a suitable register. The children want to find the appropriate tone for a formal letter to an official when the content matters to them. Presenting pupils with a range of real purposes provides children with encouragement and appropriate audiences (Protherough, 1983). In drama the real purposes are those in the drama, the pretend, which become 'real' once the pupils are involved.

The project took place in a small rural primary school with a mixed Year 3/4 class. There were 37 pupils in the class with an age range of 7–9 years old and they were of mixed ability. Outside the village is a hill, locally known as 'Crack's Hill', that was referred to in the course of the scheme of work. The pupils had experienced role-play in the classroom but not in the form of an extended serialised drama. The school had been following the framework for the National Literacy Strategy for several months and the pupils had been given the opportunity to act out scenes from the plays taught.

The Project

Giant raises environmental issues telling of a beautiful mountain that the villagers call 'Giant'. When they fail to take care of the mountain, Giant wakes up, sees the damage done and leaves. The community learn their mistakes and Giant returns.

Two weeks before the scheme took place I mounted a display on the wall as a stimulus for the pupils' learning. The display was in the form of a painting of the first scene in the book, showing the children of the village enjoying an idyllic lifestyle on the mountain (see the photo below). To place the children into the forthcoming drama I took digital photographs of them and pasted them onto the display. Some were flying kites, some picnicking under the trees, some climbing the rocks, but every pupil was included. Alongside the display were a series of questions asking the children about their life on Giant, inferring that they belonged there. The pupils were not told the purpose of the display but left to study it in their own time. They were thrilled to find themselves

A painting of the village from *Giant*.

on the mountain and spent many lunchtimes looking at the activities that were going on.

Giant is a modern day fairy story in the form of a picture book with a small amount of text. It was used as a starting point for the drama. The text from the book was used in Lessons One and Two but then the story/drama moved away from the Snape storyline. Letters and posters were modelled as the shared text in Lessons Three and Four and speaking and listening took the focus in the final session which evolved into a written or pictorial storyboard recount of the events. Some of the writing experiences were completed as draft copies whilst others were planned, drafted and finally presented.

Learning Objectives

I taught the class as a mixed ability class rather than a mixed Year group using Year 3 and Year 4 objectives. The National Literacy Framework for teaching is based on two-year cycles so the objectives for Years 3 and 4 are closely linked.

Year 3 Term 3
Text level

* to retell main points of story in sequence
* to plot a sequence of episodes modelled on a known story, as a plan for writing
* to write a first person account
* to experiment with recounting the same event

Sentence level

* to identify pronouns and understand their functions in sentences

Word level

* to continue the collection of new words

Year 4 Term 3
Text level

* to identify social, moral or cultural issues in stories – the dilemmas faced by the characters or the moral of the story, and to discuss how the characters deal with them, to locate evidence in the text

* to write critically about an issue or dilemma raised in the story, explaining the problem, alternate courses of action and evaluating the writers solution
* to explore the main issues of a story by writing a story about a dilemma and the issues it raises for the character

Sentence level

* to understand how the grammar of a sentence alters when the sentence type is altered

Word level

* to use a range of presentational skills

Assessment

For the purpose of my dissertation, I taught a series of lessons, using the story of *Red Cap* (Little Red Riding Hood), following the format set out in the National Literacy Strategy of shared text, group work and plenary. I used the writing that the children produced from these lessons to compare with writing produced during lessons using drama alongside the text *Giant*. I wished to evaluate the effects of using drama as a teaching strategy. Each writing task was differentiated to cover the range of abilities within the class. The criteria for the comparative results was that there should have been a positive improvement in the structure, vocabulary, atmosphere and emotive language used by the pupils in their writing. All of the work was written independently by the children with no adult intervention. Spellings were corrected in both the *Red Cap* and *Giant* work.

Lesson One

At the beginning of the first lesson the pupils were introduced to the text. We discussed the title, authors, read the blurb on the back cover and predicted what we thought the book might be about from the picture. I also gave the children the opportunity to discuss unfamiliar words and phrases terms such as 'ecological' and 'preserving our natural environment'.

I had previously computer written the text from pages 1–3 in large print for the children to share as a class.

Lia and her family lived in a village at the foot of a mountain. The villagers called their mountain 'Giant'. For many years they had used Giant. Giant's

plants gave them fruit. The village animals grazed on her slopes. The villagers picnicked in shady places and played in the trees. Lia and her brother,
Felix, often spent whole days on the mountain. All the children played there.

A variety of strategies were employed in the shared reading: Year 3 pupils
only, Year 4 pupils only, selected groups or individuals. Reference was made
to the local hill 'Crack's Hill' as we read the text, comparing their own experiences of living near and playing on a hill with those of the children in the
story. Again the children could discuss unfamiliar words and were encouraged
to find substitutes/synonyms that would retain meaning. I took the opportunity to exploit the word level objectives by talking about soft and hard 'G',
use of the inverted comma and the apostrophe.

I explained to the children that we were going to do some drama and that
sometimes I would be a character in the story. I made clear the signs that I
would use so that they understood when we were in or out of the drama.
When I opened my arms out the drama unfolded, when I closed them the
drama ended.

I opened the drama in the role of Lia and chatted to the village children and
drew from them what they liked to do when they played on Giant. They very
quickly fell into role and talked readily about the things they did. I noticed
that nearly all of them related their experiences to what their photographic
image was doing in the display painting. I closed the drama.

The display formed an integral part of the drama, as did the props that were
used. I pinned one end of a length of very fluid silky material to the river on
the display. It was used to represent the river. It ran from the display painting
across the classroom floor to set out the boundaries of space for the pupils. I
used the display painting to develop the children's observational and grammar
skills by asking them to name a noun such as 'tree', 'fishing rod' or 'pig' whilst
others were asked to add adjectives or verbs to the nouns. Having discussed
the images in the painting the pupils were introduced to still imaging, in which
the pupils take positions to reflect the scene in a picture. The participants are
not allowed to move unless they are touched, then they can talk and react to
the teacher.

The pupils moved into position and recreated the beautiful image of Giant, as
it is depicted in the book. Various children were asked what they were doing,
why, what they might do later and so on. The drama was closed and the

47

children repeated the observational and grammar exercises looking at the second picture in the book where the villagers are shown destroying Giant. Still imaging was used again to recreate the scene.

The pupils were divided into six groups; two higher ability (H/A), two middle ability (M/A) and two lower ability (L/A), and were given differentiated tasks for the independent group work. The H/A groups wrote comparative poetry, the M/A groups wrote comparative narratives and the L/A groups recorded before and after nouns with supporting adjectives. The plenary session was used to share work from the different groups and was an opportunity to assess the pupils' work.

> I liked Giant, I liked it very much
> I think it's real cool . . . UNTIL
> A dark cloud shone over the valley
> And the children started to MESS UP
> They started to throw sticks and stones
> And packets of litter. POLLUTION
> Came.

This example was written by Victoria, a Year 4 pupil. It showed a more mature structure compared to her poem about the wolf in *Red Cap* where she had used an acrostic structure. She has chosen to use a varied sentence length and particular choice of punctuation for impact. She has also decided to put her message across to the reader by using upper case lettering for some of the words, thus drawing attention to what she considers to be the crux of the poem. Her choice of vocabulary shows a sensitivity to the issues of pollution on Giant. She has made an impact with her words realising the subject matter in both imagined and concrete form. She builds a very heavy atmosphere through her choice of style and language particularly through her use of the sentence, 'A dark cloud shone over the valley'; this in itself has a contrast that reflects the mood of the poem. The poem is very emotive as it demands us to read and understand its message. The way that she has chosen to structure the end of the poem brings it to a crushingly sad finish as she highlights POL-LUTION in upper case letters then leaves us with the final unhappy thought, 'Came'. A single word alone that reminds us of the weight of responsibility we have for the environment.

In contrast Luke has opted for a two verse structured acrostic poem. Luke is a Year 4 pupil whose end of Year 3 assessments put him at a Level 2 for English.

Giant was very friendly
ideas from teenagers are naughty
angry parents
naughty children
tired adults.

Giant was furious
ignorant parents and preteens
annoyed preteens
nasty teenagers
tiny children follow examples.

Although he has used the safety net of an acrostic structure, the powerful choice of language shows he has engaged in the drama and transferred his thoughts onto paper. The very short sentence structures convey a strength of understanding for the subject at hand and that he is expressing thoughts and ideas that have been instilled in him probably from both parental and dramatic influences. It is interesting that he has a range of opinions that he voices in his choice of adjectives to describe adults, preteens and young children.

The next sample is written by Rame, a Year 3 pupil and I must confess, I was a little surprised at the killing of the animals but on reflection the school is a rural school where there are several farms around the village.

Rame reading her work to the class in the plenary session.

BEFORE
watching the pigs. Some people are fishing
that is what I'm going to be doing
The other day I caught 20 fish!
I am swimming in the river and catching fish.
It is hot, hot, hot and I am boiling.

AFTER
I am killing the pigs and killing the fish.
I am chopping down a tree
I am going to throw rubbish in the river.
I am killing the ducks.
It is very, very windy.
I LOVE PORK SCRATCHINGS!

Rame has firmly placed herself into the drama and this is reflected in her writing. She has a past, present and future on Giant as she describes what she is doing now – watching the pigs and swimming, what she is going to do – fish, and what she has already done – fishing and caught 20! She can 'feel' the hot sun in the before writing and this is mirrored in the ambient atmosphere she sets through her writing. However, the mood changes drastically as she launches into the after scene. The structure of her second piece of writing is very severe with the repetitive beginning of each line 'I am . . . '. Her choice of vocabulary changes the tone significantly as she 'kills' and 'chops' her way over Giant. There is a strength of emotion and determination as she ruins the countryside and relates this to the change in weather. Her final line, written in upper case lettering, is really quite macabre. Having killed the pigs she relishes the words as she pronounces, 'I LOVE PORK SCRATCHINGS!'.

Lesson Two

Lesson Two began with a reading of one of the poems from the previous day by a pupil. The rest of the class discussed its comparative language choices. This re-engaged the pupils with the drama and reinforced the purpose of nouns, adjectives and verbs. The children then read pages 6–12 and textual features were highlighted, particularly the use of speech and punctuation.

One night Giant awoke. She looked down at her coat. Then after a while she said, 'They have not cared for me. I will go away'.
While the village slept, Giant rose and strode off towards the sea. Lia woke up. Something was wrong. She ran outside.
'Giant's gone!' she cried. People ran to look. It was true.

'Whatever shall we do?' asked the villagers.
'Where will our sheep graze?' cried one.
'We will have no fruit!' wailed another.
'Where will we play?' moaned the children.

The children were asked to think of a thought Giant might have had when she woke up and saw the damage that had been done to her. They were given several lines to fall back on in case they couldn't think of one such as 'What have they done to me?'

I took the role of Giant. I lay down in the middle of the floor. I mimed Giant waking. The children spoke out the thoughts and feelings of Giant, showing their empathy at her plight. Finally, Giant walked out to sea and the drama was closed. The children then made statements to articulate the villagers' thoughts when they realised Giant had left. We practised vocal and facial expression to show the extent of our feelings. The drama was opened and I took the lead in standing up, pointing to the hole where Giant had been and made a statement. The children followed suit in the role of the villagers.

Writing in remembered role, the groups wrote diary entries. The H/A groups wrote from the perspective of Giant, the M/A groups wrote from the perspective of a villager and the L/A groups drew a character of their choice and annotated it with thought statements relevant to that character. The plenary session was dual purpose; to share work and to set the scene for the following session.

In the role of Lia, I asked the village children why they thought Giant might have left, was she right to leave or not and what we should do about it. They became very animated as they drew on their experiences from the earlier drama input. It was concluded that Lia should draft a letter to Giant for them all to look at tomorrow. The lesson ended when Lia heard her Mum calling her in and hasty arrangements were made to meet the following day at the swings.

Grace, a Year 4 pupil, has used very personal language in her diary thoughts, written as Giant. She has sustained the use of the personal pronoun 'I' throughout the passage as she writes of deep feelings of love for the villagers and how betrayed she feels by their actions. She has used some very short sentence structures to make an impact on the reader about her feelings – 'I am so puzzled. I thought they loved me so I loved them and I trusted them.' All of them reflecting the words that the pupils had used in the drama. She allows us to understand her confusion about what has happened as we look into her innermost thoughts – 'I am so, well, well you know ... heartbroken'. This hesitant way of writing; of putting her feelings into words, forms a bond with the reader. She also illustrated the writing with drawings of huge tear-drops with sad faces on them to emphasise her distress.

I am so puzzled. I just don't see why the people have been so horrible, they have ruined my coat. I am very disappointed with them. What have I done to them so they do this? I thought they loved me so I loved them. I trusted them. They have destroyed me. I did love them and I might forgive them but they did take half of me away, especially my heart. What's that black stuff in my wonderful river? They have polluted me ... OH DEAR! I am so, well, I'm well you know ... heartbroken. It's a horrible feeling when someone is so wicked to me. But I am always going to be disappointed with the villagers. They have broken my trees and scared the wildlife off. They should clean me up now.
> THEY ARE HORRIBLE PEOPLE
silly people. I trusted them. I'm disappointed in the villagers.

James, Year 3, wrote in role as a village child and he expressed his anger at Giant leaving. The passage lacks punctuation, just as thought does and the choice of language shows a defiance for the actions of Giant. The use of the word 'that' when describing Giant indicates the personal contempt James feels for her. He is very dismissive of Giant as he makes a scrap mountain that will be 'better than that old thing'. In his writing James used the language that had come up in the drama.

I feel sad, angry and cross because that Giant has gone stomping off just because I broke the branches off the trees and tipped oil in the river and nows she's gone stomping off I can make my own mountain out of scraps and that will be better than that old thing I can run around on scraps.

Lesson Three

Lesson Three began with me in role as Lia greeting the children as they arrived at the swings. I chatted to them as if they were my village chums, joking and gossiping about our families and what has happened so far to reinforce their learning. It is at this point that we move away from the Juliet and Charles Snape story and the children begin to claim ownership of the events.

Remaining in role, I show the village children the letter that I have written and use it as the shared text. The format, vocabulary, tone of the letter and grammar are totally inappropriate. The villagers read the letter and discuss why and where it needs to be amended. We discussed how it should be structured, the degree of formality that should be used and the type of language that is required for different purposes of letters such, as in this case, persuasive vocabulary. A new letter was written on the board with the children debating on the content and style. On completing the letter, which provided a model, Lia suggested that perhaps it might be a good idea if they all wrote a letter to Giant so that she could see that they all really wanted her to come back.

All of the children wrote letters to Giant and the work was differentiated by outcome. The plenary session was used to read out some of the letters which were then rolled up and put into empty milk bottles to be sent out to sea to reach Giant. The whole lesson was in role and ended in a prediction activity about what the villagers thought Giant might do when she read the letters. Arrangements were made to meet the next day as various children were called home by their mothers.

> Dear my best friend Giant
> I am very ashamed of my behaviour. I'm sorry I have made you go away in disappointment of me. I apologise also for polluting your wonderful, clean, blue river and for spraying graffiti on your magnificent, tall trees. Every time I look at the hole in the middle of our houses it makes me want to cry. If I ask you, you would not want to forgive me. If you come back, which I hope you will, I would try my hardest to change the drastic things I've done. I do love you. xxxxxx
>
> Yours sincerely
>
> I'm sorry

Grace's style of writing is sincerely formal but friendly, 'Dear my best friend Giant' coupled with 'Yours sincerely'. Not only has she apologised for all of the awful things she has done as a villager, but she has thought from Giant's perspective by suggesting that Giant '... wouldn't want to forgive me'. She hasn't made the assumption that Giant would return because of her letter but hopes that she will. She has drawn on her prior drama experiences of taking the role of villager and Giant.

Lesson Four

Lesson Four began in role as I, Lia, excitedly called to the children that I had received a letter from Giant. The letter became the shared text where different groups of children read it depending on ability levels. It contained some quite challenging vocabulary and figurative language.

Giant
The Sea
England
January 20, 1999

The Children
Smallton
England

Dear Children,
Thank you for the letters that you sent to me. I am not happy because I am not in my beloved home but I was so upset that you had all ruined my beautiful coat that I had to leave. I have wept rivers of sadness at how you have treated me. My face has been disfigured so badly by the paint that has been sprayed upon it that I cannot bear to look at my reflection in the sea. My trees are broken and feel crushed inside because of the tears to their bodies. My life blood, the river, flows slowly as the blackness seeps at my energy. I have been betrayed and my heart cries in agony at the pain that you have inflicted upon me by scorching my body with your fires.
You write that you are sorry and that you want forgiveness but how can I be sure that you mean this? I need to look into your faces and peer into the windows of your souls to see if you really are sorry. I need to know that you will not do these awful things to me again if I return and that you will never, never take me for granted as you have done in the past.

Yours sincerely,
Giant

The villagers discussed the layout of the letter which was different from the format they had used (the address was on the left hand side suitable for a window envelope). They were encouraged to use a variety of reading strategies to understand the meaning of some of the metaphors and similes. They needed to infer what Giant wanted from them by reading the clues in the letter. An example being, 'I want to look into the windows of your souls'. Having established that Giant wanted to meet them, Lia asked the villagers what they could do to make sure everyone knew about the meeting. They decided to make posters. Lia showed them some posters she had found to model as examples. They discussed the details they would need to use for the posters, highlighting large fonts, eyecatching, informative – when, where and why, and for whom they are designed. The task was for each child to produce a poster, still in role.

Shared text

The plenary session was an assessment opportunity for me and the children, to evaluate each others' posters against the criteria that had been previously discussed. Several children were nominated to pin the posters up around the village (school grounds and building) and plans were made to meet on the beach the following day.

Lesson Five

The format of the final lesson was changed so that the pupils' speaking and listening skills could be assessed through the context of the meeting. I set the scene for the children – we were on the beach waiting for Giant to come. I explained that I would take the role of Giant and they would be the villagers. I nominated one pupil to be Lia and to open the drama by calling to Giant. Before starting we discussed the sort of things we might say to her and what we might need to promise so that she would come back.

The villagers sat on the beach looking out to sea. Giant had her back to them and heard Lia calling her. She refused to turn round and needed encouragement from the villagers to do so. She looked hurt and upset as she turned around and moved toward the beach and the villagers. She asked them what they wanted and the children were encouraged to use persuasive language to get her back. It was an opportunity to reinforce all of the work that had been covered during the week and to draw individual responses from the children. All of the villagers had something to say because they had all experienced the drama input. Eventually Giant agreed to come back, but only on the condition that they write down everything that has happened to pass down to future generations. Only then could she be sure that she would never be taken for granted again.

Giant indicated to the villagers that she wanted to return to her resting place and they moved into a circle. She walked to the spot, lay down and went to sleep. While I was doing this I narrated the end of the story. After several seconds, I sat up and closed the drama. Remaining on the floor we discussed what had happened and what Giant wanted them to do. We recounted all of the events that had happened during the week and the children were given their differentiated writing tasks. The H/A and M/A groups planned sequenced written recounts whilst the L/A groups planned sequenced pictorial storyboards. The plenary session was used to discuss and reinforce the events of the week.

The National Literacy Strategy allocates one week per term for extended writing activities and this was used the following week so that the pupils could continue planning, drafting and final copying their recounts.

In Conclusion

Having completed the week of drama and marked all of the work I was surprised at the end results. The majority of the writing showed a significant improvement compared to the *Red Cap* work. This was particularly evident where the children had written in the role of a character – diary thoughts and letter writing. The language was highly emotive and there was a real sense of it being a very personal experience. The structure and language use in the writing appeared to have moved onto a higher plane in that there was a subconscious desire to make the message clear to the reader, particularly visible in the poetry comparing the two scenes. The results show that the majority of children were aware of the audiences for which they were writing and responded appropriately, thus supporting the views of Protherough (1983), that giving children a range of 'real' purposes for writing provides them with encouragement and appropriate audiences.

The Department of Education and Science (1990) indicated that drama was beneficial in improving literacy in all abilities. The use of differentiated tasks gave all pupils the opportunity to achieve success. Overall, the standard of work did improve and the evidence suggests that the lower ability children did appear to produce more meaningful writing. The research of Vygotsky (1978) and later McMaster (1998), indicates that play has a fundamental impact on aspects of emergent literacy, and it would appear that the use of drama influences the literacy learning of pupils.

After the scheme had finished I questioned the pupils to find out if they felt the drama had helped them in their writing, 80% of them said that they found writing easier because of the drama input. This has huge implications on the teaching of literacy to young children. Evidence gathered reveals the strength of feeling and engagement in the drama is reflected in the subsequent writing. The children used emotive language that had been thought out very carefully before being committed to paper. They had chosen and were developing a wide range of vocabulary, strengthening their work by the use of powerful verbs and adjectives. The structure of their writing reflected the mood of the words they were using, developing a maturity of style that had not previously been present.

The whole experience was motivating for both myself and the children. They loved being able to act out parts of the story and having the chance to make important decisions about what should happen next. It really seemed to matter what they wrote and how it was written because of the consequences it would have on the drama. From my point of view, I had the opportunity to observe how various pupils approached and tackled the 'problems' that arose within the context of the drama and could then address the issues that arose during the more formal aspects of the lesson. If nothing else I hope that my experience, as a novice teacher and dramatist, will make the thought of doing drama a little less scary because as the old adage goes . . . if I can do it then anyone can!

Bibliography

Protherough, *Encouraging Writing*, Methuen, 1983.

Kitson, N. & Spiby, I., Drama 7–11: *Developing Primary Teaching Skills*, Routledge, 1997.

Booth, D., 'What coyotes have to say: Writing from remembered role' in David Booth and Jonothan Neelands (eds) (1998) *Writing in Role: Classroom Projects Connecting Writing and Drama*, Caliburn Enterprises Inc, 1998.

Vygotsky, L. S., *Mind in Society*, M.I.T. Press, 1978.

McMaster, J. C., 'Doing Literature: Using Drama to Build Literacy' in *Reading Teacher*, April 1998, Vol. 51 Issue 7, p 574, 1998.

Department of Education and Science, *Aspects of Primary Education – The Teaching and Learning of Drama*, HMSO, 1990.

Lesson Guide

Resources Giant text, plain paper, pens, pencils, crayons, dictionaries, thesauruses, letters from Giant and Lia, examples of posters.

Lesson One

* **Shared reading:** Introduce text to children, discuss cover, blurb on back, author. What might this book be about? – prediction. Children (groups/individuals) to read pages 6–8 and discuss any unfamiliar words or terms, highlight use of soft/hard 'G'. Show children the picture/display. Explain drama conventions – open/close book; still imaging.
* **Shared text:** Children in circle – look at 'beautiful' picture (pages 2–3) and

Year 3	•	Year 4
W12		W15
T12		
		T1, 8
S2		

name a noun e.g. 'river'; adjective e.g. 'flowing'; verb e.g. 'fishing'. Define the area for the imagined river, foot of Giant etc. to be.

* **Still image 1:** Children are to be the villagers on the mountainside having a wonderful time. Remind them to remain still as a picture in the book. They can only come to life when they are touched. Ask individuals what they are doing on the mountain, do they play here often etc. Encourage them to take ownership of the drama by asking questions about their family and likes and dislikes. Close the page and children return to circle.

* **Shared text:** Look at picture depicting pollution of Giant. Identify features as before.

* **Still image 2:** Use as above. Close page and regroup class. Discuss what they have done in the drama and encourage them to make comparisons. Refer to synonyms and antonyms. Allocate work.

* **Comparative language tasks:** Differentiated task to compare pictures 1 and 2. Group A: comparison poetry; Group B: before/after narrative; Group C: classifying nouns with supporting adjectives.

* **Plenary:** One child from each group to read comparison work.

Lesson Two

Year 3
W12
T12
S2
Year 4
T1, 2, 11

* **Shared reading:** Choose one piece of poetry written by a pupil (enlarged onto A3) and let writer read aloud to class, discuss choice of words and if it compares the scenes well. This will re-establish the children to the drama. Return to *Giant* text, to see Giant wake up (groups/individuals).

* **Shared text:** Discuss unfamiliar words, use of speech marks and punctuation to denote tone of expression. Synonyms for 'said'. Practice saying speech following punctuation. Discuss how Giant must feel – relate to how they feel if someone has done something horrible to them.

* **Teacher in role:** Open drama – Teacher in role as Giant – lie on floor waking up and saying 'What have they done to me?'. Then leave, walking into the sea.

* **Statementing 1:** Children to offer thought statements that Giant might be thinking. Give them a 'safety net' by allowing them to repeat the sentence 'What have they ...?' Allow time for them to think of original ideas. Prompt where necessary. Close drama. Return to circle.

* **Statementing 2:** Open drama – Taking role of villagers and following ideas from text, children to walk up to empty hole and say sentences relating to how villagers feel. Close drama.

* **Diary thoughts task:** Differentiated tasks taking the perspective of character. Group A: Writing in role of Giant; Group B: Writing in role of villager;

Group C: Character statement web (sketch character and annotate with thoughts).

* **Plenary:** One child from each group to share writing/sketching.

* **Teacher in role:** Open drama – As Lia, 'gossip' to children about why Giant has left. Involve children by being friendly and asking opinions. Encourage them to suggest Lia writes Giant a letter asking her to come back. Close drama by announcing you can hear Mum calling you in and decide on a place where you can all meet in the morning.

Lesson Three

* **Teacher in role:** Open page. Greet children as if you have arrived at the destination as arranged from the night before. Place them into the role of village children by referring to what they might have done last night e.g. 'Charlie, I saw you running home last night from my house window. You were out late, I bet your Mum went mad when you got home ...' Produce the letter that Lia wrote from your pocket or bag. Ask children to read it and see if they think it's OK.

* **Shared reading:** Children (groups/individuals) to read the letter that Lia composed to send to Giant. Letter is totally inappropriate using demanding sentences and incorrect use of grammar and punctuation.

* **Shared text/writing:** Discuss type of language used in Lia's letter and write a model letter with the children. Encourage them to offer suggestions on how to change the text from Lia's letter to make it sound more persuasive. Discuss how you, the children, should structure the letter. Maintain role-play and suggest that everyone should write a letter to Giant to persuade her to come back. Discuss content, what would they include in their letters?

* **Letter writing task – still in role:** All children to write a letter to Giant, differentiated by outcome.

* **Plenary – still in role:** Select different ability children to read their letters and ask others if they were Giant would they have been persuaded to come back. Roll up the letters and put them into empty milk bottles so they can be floated out to Giant. Arrange to meet next day.

Year 3
W12
Year 4 • S3 S12
T11

59

Lesson Four

* **Teacher in role:** As Lia, excitedly call to the children that you have had a letter back from Giant. Ask 'villagers' if they heard anything last night, whether they think Giant popped back to deliver it etc. – this will bring them back into the drama.

Year 3 •	Year 4
W12	**W15**
	T1

* **Shared reading – in role:** Children (groups/individuals) to read letter from Giant.
* **Shared text – in role:** Encourage children to use grammatical knowledge to infer meaning from text. Ask them to describe what Giant means when she uses figurative language. Discuss what she might mean by wanting to 'peer into the windows of their souls' and how she could do this. Guide them into arranging for a meeting with her. How can we advertise the proposed meeting? – posters! Show children some examples of posters and discuss poster presentation format. Decide where, when, how.
* **Designing posters – in role:** All children to make a poster notifying rest of village about the meeting with Giant.
* **Plenary:** Children given opportunity to show posters and evaluate. Lia suggests they pin them up around the village (school/grounds) – close page.

Lesson Five

Year 3 • Year 4
S2   W15
T1, 10, 22   T1

* **Setting the scene:** Day of the meeting. Tell children that you are going to take the role of Giant and they are going to be the villagers. Nominate one child to take the role of Lia.
* **Role play:** Children to arrange themselves on floor as if they are at a meeting, Giant stands out at sea. Drama opens when Lia calls to Giant. Villagers have to use persuasive language to encourage Giant to come back to her place. Giant resists, expressing her feelings about how betrayed she feels and asking what the villagers will do to make amends. Giant agrees to come back but under the proviso that everyone will write about what has happened, so that it can be passed down the generations ensuring the awful things never happen again. Giant walks into village, lies down and goes to sleep. Quietly sit up, gather children around and recall the week's events.
* **Recount writing:** Differentiated recounts sequencing events – planning stage: Groups A & B – narrative of events; Group C – pictorial storyboard.
* **Plenary:** Discuss and evaluate planning.
* **Extended writing:** Develop recount writing over following week.

Whoosh, Bang and Whiz!
◦using◦
The Firework-maker's Daughter
by Philip Pullman

John Miller is Head of Drama and Music at Nicholas Hawksmoor Primary School, Towcester, Northamptonshire. He has worked extensively with the Royal Opera Company's Education Team, and recently collaborated with his pupils to write and perform an opera.

Throughout my 25 years in teaching there have been many changes to the style, curriculum content and organisation of my chosen profession, and I have instigated not a few myself having trained as a Music teacher and then discovered my true calling in Drama in Education and Theatre. I am very fortunate to work in a school which actively encourages teaching in all the arts and aims to provide as much learning as possible through first-hand experience. Drama is a great tool for first-hand experience as it involves the children in 'real' but fictitious situations and gives them a 'reason' for knowing.

The coming of the Literacy Hour has caused many to think that a lot of that 'first-hand experience' and 'exciting' teaching was going to go out of the window, but this only spurred me on to try to find a solution to this problem, to show that teaching with Drama in literacy could work.

The Project

The project was a previous series of drama activities adapted to fulfil a range of literacy objectives, and to run according to the Literacy Hour framework. I was keen not to sacrifice the quality of the drama, and to ensure that the drama objectives were also maintained.

I first chose a set of lessons based on the opening two chapters of the novel *The Firework-maker's Daughter* which I knew the children of Year 4 would enjoy because I had used the book the previous year. It had been a great success. It is a wonderful book that has enchanted children. It is not necessary to have the book to use this lesson plan, but I do recommend it as an exciting read.

The book is set in a mythical eastern country. Lila, who has been brought up by her father, desperately wants to be a firework-maker but she is a girl and her father, being a traditionalist, does not think it a fitting job for her. Every firework-maker has to make the perilous journey to face the terrifying fire-fiend, Razvani. Lila determines to make this journey to learn the secrets with the help of her friends, Chulak and Hamlet the love-sick elephant. Of course she is successful in overcoming great odds.

I am constantly amazed by the acceptance of children to the world of drama; their readiness to accept and suspend disbelief as long as they know, 'this is going to be fun and I might enjoy it!'. It gives an added thrill to a lesson, teacher's kicks, when the children plough in with gusto. I do mean *all* the children, as even the quiet ones will 'be' an audience with all their might. So, to that end, entering a classroom on a Monday with a new set of ideas under my belt is exciting and scary. Even more butterflies because this was my first major attempt to marry Literacy Hour with drama. I wanted it to be a big success.

Learning Objectives

Word level

* to identify and consolidate the spelling of suffixes working from root words e.g. 'ly', 'ing', 'ful', 'ive', 'ic'
* to identify misspelt words in own writing
* to practise new spellings regularly by 'look, say, cover, write, check' strategy.

Sentence level

* to consolidate the use of appropriate adjectives and powerful verbs
* to introduce the adverb modifying a verb
* to explore how adverbs help to explain people's actions and motives in story
* to explore the use of connectives in an argument.

Text level

* to investigate how characters are built up from small details and how we respond to them
* to evaluate adverts for their impact, appeal and honesty focusing in particular on how information about the product is presented

* to establish that the dilemmas characters face have a foundation in their past
* to establish that events in a story have to be sorted chronologically
* to identify social, moral or cultural issues in stories
* to consolidate work on play writing
* to look at the dilemmas that are created in stories and to explore how a lot is said in a few words
* to look beyond the words for meaning, to read between the lines (subtext)

Assessment

Assessment was carried out through a range a specific tasks:

1 The written content of the fliers in Lessons 1 and 2 – powerful verbs/adjectives and adverbs used
2 The appropriate identifying of adverbs to describe how the characters felt and responded to the situations throughout
3 The written subtext to the script, how it was to be performed and said, and its performances and criticisms
4 The oral use of connectives in reply to Lalchlan's arguments in the Forum Theatre (see below)
5 The accuracy of the spelling of the adverbs, power verbs and adjectives within all above, especially the use of the suffixes 'ly' and 'ing'.

Lesson One

The announcement, 'Could Michelle and Emma move their table and Stephen could you move . . .' is enough to set an excited buzz within the class and when arranged we're off. The children that I teach are already prepared for Teacher in Role or as we say, 'Mr Miller becoming people', so it is no surprise when I address them as an unknown character, Lalchlan, and they work out 'who' they are talking to and 'who' they are.

I had struck on the idea that Lalchlan, Lila's father in the book, was a great character for Teacher in Role because of his quiet fatherly authority. I had also decided that he had lost his glasses and therefore would need help with reading a letter from the Headteacher of Nicholas Hawksmoor Primary School requesting information on certain fireworks mentioned in the first chapter of the book. I had prepared the following letter:

School Address
Date

Lalchlan Fireworks & Daughter,
A Thousand Miles Ago,
East of the Jungle,
South of the Mountains.

Dear Sir,

We are holding our annual Fireworks Party on Guy Fawkes Night, the 5th of November, and we are thinking of buying our fireworks from you as your fame has spread far and wide.

We are especially interested in the following fireworks:
1. Leaping Monkeys
2. Golden Sneezes
3. Crackle Dragons
4. Tumbling Demons
5. Shimmering Coins.

We would like an in depth description of each of these fireworks to help us decide whether to buy yours or some from Brock's. We want to know:
1. How long do each of these fireworks last?
2. What noises do they make and how loud?
3. What colours and shapes do they make and how bright are they?
4. How safe are they and are there any special instructions about lighting them safely?
5. Any other special descriptions which would help us make up our minds, including how much fun people have had watching them?

We hope to hear from you very soon as there is little time left to decide.

Yours sincerely

(Headteacher)

This seemed an obvious but very effective way of getting the class to read shared text but still be within the drama. Built into the text of the letter are the list of fireworks and various hooks which would help to produce the work ahead, and were aimed at providing a context for the work of the lesson. They were being prepared to produce descriptive work using powerful words.

The letter immediately places the children in the role of experts. They are those who know about fireworks, but I wanted to take this responsibility a stage further by creating experts within experts. So, in role as Lalchlan, I asked which workers had been working on which fireworks. This produced groups of children who could then concentrate on one firework be it Leaping Monkeys or Tumbling Demons. This also brought more commitment to the drama. As most children have some affinity with fireworks and their effects it was not long before children were coming up with words like 'loud bangs' and 'crashes' and 'sparkling'. But I wanted to push further than that so, as Lalchlan, I announced that these descriptions would not be any better than the other firework-makers and encouraged my expert workers to go and light their fireworks and observe them with care and to come up with just the right words. 'Not only the colours but HOW the fireworks exploded – beautifully, suddenly etc. Let's have some great adverbs and remember we have to have this done quickly or we will miss out on a big order which will keep you in work for weeks.'

I found that challenging the children in this way spurred them to work with purpose and a will. I have also found that if I use technical language like adverb, and explain implicitly through the role, the children accept it. After all they are in the drama, and to do their job they must have knowledge of the language which will best describe their fireworks.

The use of mime to explore the effect of these fireworks was very important to the lesson as it focused the children's minds on the effect. I narrated, 'The workers went to try their own particular fireworks. They carefully lit the blue touch paper and retired to a safe distance', and so on. This use of mime and narration produced great concentration and the children were soon coming up with powerful words. Here are just two typical ideas:

> **Connie**: Leaping monkeys are wonderfully explosive. They jump spectacularly.
> **Daniel**: Twirling evilly the Tumbling Demons howl around.

At the instruction of Lalchlan the workers then went off to write adverts to be included in the letter to the headteacher while I, still in role as Lalchlan, worked with a less able group. I found that keeping up the Teacher in Role made the work more fun and I could challenge the children much more through the role. 'Get this right and there will be overtime to make all these fireworks.' The children just seemed to accept the instruction about word work as part of the drama.

Lalchlan: That's a good adjective Shea. It describes the coins perfectly.

or

Lalchlan: You've written an adverb Lorna. Look at the ly. That helps to describe it clearly. He's sure to want some now.

In the plenary I kept up the role of Lalchlan and got the children to read/perform their fliers. As we watched, I muttered things like, 'Oh yes, good adverb', 'Oo, excellent description', 'That ought to sell the fireworks', 'Did you notice …?' It finished on this positive note although I noticed that the 'independent' work was not at such a high standard as was expected – the next lesson would need to deal with that problem. I ended the lesson with a speech from Lalchlan thanking his workers for a great day's work and noting that as the letter is going to a headteacher in Britain he hopes that all the spellings are correct including the 'ings' and 'lys' because headteachers in Britain are renowned for their insistence on brilliant spelling. Unfortunately, Lalchlan can't tell himself because he has not yet found his spectacles.

Lesson Two

I planned to raise the standards of the workers' firework fliers. I decided to do this by introducing the central character of the story, Lila as a contrast. She is a headstrong girl with a need to be a success and I could use the role to be critical of the workers' efforts.

The lesson began in the usual quiet, calm way with the teacher in role as Lila, praising the workers on their firework-making skills. However, she continued by waving yesterday's work in her hand and remonstrating with the workers, 'How did they expect the business to survive! My father is too kind hearted! The truth is if these fliers are not improved – no more business, no more jobs! We need adverts that will sell our fireworks to that fussy headteacher!'

This role was a huge contrast to yesterday's well-meaning character and sharply focused the children's minds back into the drama and to the purpose for writing the fliers. It gave them a real challenge and created a tension without which the drama would not run. The rest of Lila's speech went on to gee up the workers and ended with Lila demonstrating what a good flier was all about. I showed them a flier from a local company. As Lila, I used it to show how powerful verbs, adjectives and adverbs can be employed to best effect and will lead into the best use of powerful words and modifying adverbs for the fliers. At the end of Lila's speech I placed a challenge. She expected to see and hear much better fliers in 20 minutes' time.

As before, I kept the role going throughout the group and independent work except this time the role of Lila gave me more scope for encouraging rigour, depth of thought and accuracy. The children approached the role with more respect and wanted to gain approval:

> **Daniel**: Lila, is this word 'tremendously' a good word to use?
> **Lila**: A great adverb. What firework does it go with? What does it do 'tremendously'?
> **Daniel**: Crackle Dragons and it explodes tremendously.
> **Lila**: Well done! Father will be pleased with that in the flier!

Of course I also kept up the challenge through the role during this work.

The Plenary, as Monday, was a run through of the fliers but this time they had to meet the approval of Lila a much more rigorous critic, sitting with arms crossed and a stern expression, therefore adding to the tension of the performance and adding to the need for the workers to have improved the fliers.

Lesson Three

I decided to take a completely different tack on the next day to show another side to Lila's character, and pursue further textual learning. I wanted them to realise that dilemmas characters face have their foundation in their past. There are some of which they had no control over, some of which they did.

Seeing as the children knew a bit about the characters from the first two days I decided to explore these characters with more rigour and depth and also to explore their past. I know of no better way of engaging children of this age with character than using drama. It provides an active experience of the challenge and tension of drama. It gives them a need and a desire to explore. I also found, as in the past, that there is a spell cast by a prepared teacher. A good story must be revealed well. (It's the way you tell 'em!)

I debated with myself whether to use a Role on the Wall convention to start the text level part of the lesson as a shared writing exercise. This would produce some good powerful adjectival work but I decided against this because of the time constraints and because I wanted to get to the heart of my objective. I decided on a shared reading of the first three pages of the book:

A thousand miles ago, in a country east of the jungle and south of the mountains, there lived a firework-maker called Lalchlan and his daughter Lila. Lalchlan's wife had died when Lila was young. The child was a cross little thing, always crying and refusing her food, but Lalchlan built a cradle for her in the corner of the workshop, where she could see the sparks play and listen to the fizz and crackle of the gunpowder. Once she was out of her cradle, she toddled around the workshop laughing as the fire flared and the sparks danced. Many a time she burnt her little fingers, but Lalchlan splashed water on them and kissed her better, and soon she was playing again. When she was old enough to learn, her father began to teach her the art of making fireworks. She began with little Crackle Dragons, six on a string. Then she learned how to make Leaping Monkeys, Golden Sneezes and Java Lights.

Soon she was making all the simple fireworks, and thinking about more complicated ones.

One day she said, 'Father, if I put some flowers of salt in a Java Light instead of cloud powder, what would happen?'

'Try it and see,' he said.

So she did. Instead of burning with a steady green glimmer, it sprayed out wicked little sparks, each of which turned a somersault before going out.

'Not bad, Lila,' said Lalchlan. 'What are you going to call it?'

'Mmm . . . Tumbling Demons,' she said.

'Excellent! Make a dozen and we'll put them into the new year festival display.'

The tumbling demons were a great success and so were the shimmering coins that Lila invented next. As time went on she learned more and more of her father's art, until one day she said, 'Am I a proper firework-maker now?'

'No, no,' he said. 'By no means. Ha! You don't know the start of it.'

I wrote the text on my board the night before but you could have it on sheets for the children. I then began a negotiation/discussion with the children about whether Lila did, 'know the start of it'. We decided to find out if she did. This was my teacher decision with the co-operation of the class.

We began by brainstorming the types of incidents that might have happened to Lila in a firework factory, creating a context for her. The children through suggesting these ideas, began to gain a deeper connection with the story and its characters. This gave them more ownership of the story. To deepen this involvement we next used a ritual. Every child took on the role of Lila and thought of one memory, one already discussed or an original one if they could. They stated, one at a time, 'I remember when I was . . .', then described an incident and its consequence. One example spoken seriously by Rohanna was,

'The crackle dragon pot overfilled and I burnt my hand and I had to go to hospital'.

These moments built up a picture of the past and gave the children lots of working material for the rest of the lesson. This proved an excellent way of working because, when independent work came the children had lots of material to call on. I then asked the children to go into groups of three or four and pick their favourite incidents from Lila's past and arrange themselves into still images to depict the incident. Then we put them into context by writing descriptive captions for each of them with the age Lila was when the incident occurred. We then moved the images into a piece of theatre. The images were seen as photographs in a family album. The children order their pictures chronologically. Teacher in role as Lalchlan, with a selected child as Lila, sat together in a scene depicting them looking through the family album reminiscing about Lila growing up. Lalchlan would turn a page and say for example, 'Oh, yes I remember when you were three ...', and the children would recognise their group and form the appropriate picture. This did need to be done twice because a group of less able children missed their cue but this was a learning experience for them and they were correct the second time. At the end of the last time the child in the role of Lila, who had been prepared earlier spoke the line, 'Am I a proper firework-maker now?' and I replied with Lalchlan's words in a very angry voice 'No, no. By no means. Ha! You don't know the start of it yet'.

This gave a hook for the next day's lesson creating tension and expectation, especially when Lorna sidled up to me and asked, 'Why's he angry?' I replied, 'We'll find out tomorrow'. There was an, 'Awh!' of disappointment from the class but they are used to me doing this in many areas of the curriculum.

The independent work was writing the memories of Lila in poetic/caption form and we called it, 'I remember'. In the guided work we explored these descriptions and the feelings of the characters of Lila through powerful adjectives, verbs and especially how things were done, bringing out the modifying adverbs and their endings.

The Plenary looked at the family album again but from the specific angle of how Lila and Lalchlan behaved – anxiously, angrily, happily and so on.

Lesson Four

I began the next day's lesson with the text of the letter from Lila to her father which appears in the book. We read the letter as a shared reading text and then a few children read it in different ways for example, a game of adverbs was played in which each child read it according to the instruction of an adverb – loudly, quietly, sadly, angrily and so on. The children then commented on which would sound correct and some even offered combinations of adverbs to try such as quietly and angrily. This was an example of an idea coming in the lesson.

We then turned to the dialogue from the previous lesson. The children divided into pairs to explore the possible continuation of this conversation knowing that Lila was angry enough after it to sign herself, 'Your ex-daughter Lila'. After a while we discussed the types of words used by the characters in their dialogues. The children came up with, 'But, but ...', 'So!', 'I don't want to!' They then went away to have another go at the argument.

As a result of this pair work exploration, when the children came to try forum theatre to agree on the dialogue, they had a wealth of material to work with. In forum theatre children volunteer to 'perform' their scenes in front of the class and the others get a chance, after the scene, to come in and try their own versions swapping roles as need be. As the children did this much discussion ensued. They tried out one idea after another. The selection of words and the mode of delivery were dealt with in stunning detail. I find forum theatre a very powerful tool to work with in the classroom as it gives the children the power to try out different ways of solving a dilemma as they search for what is most appropriate. We knew whatever we set up had to convincingly result in Lila's letter.

Independent work engaged children writing the scene the way they thought it would go giving them a chance to concretise their version of events. The guided group worked with me on powerful adjectives, verbs and adverbs to describe the feelings of the characters in the scene with an emphasis on adverbs describing how the characters said things and behaved.

In the Plenary the children shared some of their scripts and the guided group commented on 'how' the characters acted and expressed themselves by identifying suitable adverbs such as 'angrily', 'sadly'. We noted the spelling of these words on the board.

Lesson Five

I took as a shared text a scripted version of the conversation which Lila and her father had in the novel:

Lila: Am I a proper Firework-Maker now?

Lalchlan: No, no, by no means. Ha! You don't know the start of it. What are the ingredients of fly-away powder?

Lila: I don't know.

Lalchlan: And where do you find thunder-grains?

Lila: I've never heard of thunder-grains.

Lalchlan: How much Scorpion Oil do you put in a Krakatoa Fountain?

Lila: A teaspoonful?

Lalchlan: What? You'd blow the whole city up. You've got a lot to learn yet. Do you really want to be a Firework-Maker, Lila?

Lila: Of course I do! It's the only thing I really want!

Lalchlan: I was afraid so. It's my own fault. What was I thinking of? I should have sent you to my sister Jembavati to bring you up as a dancer. This is no place for a girl, now I come to think of it, and, and just look at you! Your hair's a mess, your fingers are burned and stained with chemicals, your eyebrows are scorched … How am I going to find a husband for you when you look like that?

Lila: A husband?

Lalchlan: Well, of course! You don't imagine you can stay here forever, do you?

[**Lila** *leaves her father standing there*]

After reading this as a class I asked for volunteers to perform their versions written the day before in independent work and a short discussion ensued about the merits of each. All the children thought their versions were better! I asked them if it was because they thought that they had shown more emotion in performing their scripts. A resounding 'Yes!' was the reply.

At this point I had decided that I would insist that they now rehearse Philip Pullman's version of the script and put all the emotions into how they said the words. I said, 'Think how to say the words. What adverbs would describe how to express yourself?' They came up with adverbs such as 'eagerly', 'happily', 'sadly', 'angrily', 'questioningly', 'grumpily' and even 'disappointedly' and 'dejectedly'. The children then rehearsed the exact lines as a performance. I found from observing the rehearsals that children's understanding of the subtext was beginning to produce authentic and even moving performances.

The children in pairs noted on their scripts how they would say each line and how they would act and react. This led to the Plenary in which volunteers read their scripts. I would then ask the obvious question, 'did they follow their adverbs?' and slipped in the word 'subtext' which was immediately questioned by Lorna. I explained that this new word meant what is really meant or felt behind a line. I demonstrated by saying, 'You're a very nice boy, Tom!' in a loud and fierce voice. I asked the children what I said and how I said it and what I really meant! They got it.

It had been a very satisfying week because I had mostly done what I had set out to do – Drama and the Literacy Hour. It could be done but needed a lot of planning. This trial run gave me great heart and I am now trying a series of lessons where we explore poetry, character, description and costuming. So far it's going well and I have roped my colleague into trying it as well. She concluded during the drama and poetry sessions, 'Each poem we do like this, the children think is the best we've done!'

Lesson Guide

Resources: *The Firework-maker's Daughter* by Philip Pullman, pens, pencils, large coloured felt pens, A4 paper, a firework or other advertising flier, letter from the Headteacher, sugar paper, a copy of the letter written by Lila in Chapter Two, a scripted version of the confrontation between Lila and Lalchlan.

Lesson One

Year 4 • Term 1
W7, S3, 4
T24

- ◈ Time: 1 hour and 10 minutes
- ◈ **Teacher in role:** As Lalchlan, with a letter from the Headteacher which he can't read because he has mislaid his spectacles. Children in role as the workers at his firework factory have to read the letter. Teacher in role asks for the adverts for each of fireworks which must be produced quickly.
- ◈ **Small group mime:** In firework groups children describe as they light, stand well back and 'observe' what 'happens'. They explain what they look like, the strength of them and how they perform. 'Scribes' in each group write down good appropriate adjectives, powerful verbs and useful adverbs for using as an advertising flier.
- ◈ **Independent and group guided work – adverbs:** The teacher works with Group A on their lists of words sorting into appropriate adjectives looking especially at those with the 'ing' suffixes, discussing power verbs and why

they are powerful and adverbs of how and their suffix, 'ly'. Teacher can remain in role as Lalchlan for fun and to keep the children involved with the drama. The independent groups work on the adverts for their particular fireworks.

* **Plenary – performance:** The children as workers perform their adverts, if they wish, or read them out while teacher in role as Lalchlan comments favourably or otherwise, and encourages other groups to identify the good adjectives, power verbs and adverbs.

Lesson Two

* **Time:** 1 hour
* **Teacher in role:** As Lila. The children in role as the workers. Lila congratulates the workers on their skill as firework-makers and then criticises their abilities in writing adverts. She draws children's attention to the use of appropriate adjectives, powerful verbs and adverbs in some fliers. Lila provides a list of what is needed for a good flier for workers to use as a guide.
* **Independent and guided group work:** Similar to Lesson One though the focus group is Group B.
* **Plenary – teacher in role:** Lila presents the prepared reply letter from her Father, written of course by her, and the letter is read with groups inserting their improved adverts, into the format. Lila congratulates the workers on a much improved set of adverts which she will now send off to the school.

S3, 4
T16, 17, 24

73

Lesson Three

* **Time:** 1 hour
* **Text:** Teacher reads chapter one, pages 1–2 and the top of page 3 up to ' "No, no," he said, "By no means. Ha! You don't know the start of it." ' (Copies of this for the children.)
* **Brainstorm:** What it would be like to grow up in a firework-maker's workshop. What could happen? What kind of dangers etc? Teacher scribes the possible incidents asking when/at what age did this happen?
* **Ritual:** Each child makes up a memory: 'I remember when I was three the …'. The children make an appropriate gesture to go with the memory, e.g. holding their arm and saying, 'I remember when I was four the Jumping Jacks jumped up my sleeve and burnt my arm.' This helps the children to form a great deal of working material for the next part of the work.
* **Still image and captions:** The photo album. In groups of three or four children decide on a memory to portray as a still image photo. Agree:

W2, 7
T3
Term 2
T13

1. What age Lila was;

2. Where the incident takes place;

3. Who took the photo and why.

Children caption the still images with a title and an age. The teacher and a child as Lalchlan and Lila, look through the 'photo album' with teacher in role leading by turning the pages and saying such things as 'O look, remember that? You were only three and . . .' etc. The appropriate group then form the 'photograph' in front of Lalchlan and Lila. Rehearse a couple of times until it flows well. Add lines at end. Lila: 'Am I a proper firework-maker now?' Lalchlan: 'No, no, By no means. Ha! You don't know the start of it', in an angry voice.

- **Independent and guided group work – writing memories:** The independent work that follows this is written work in role where the workers write out their memories of Lila as she grew up. The focus guided group C look at the use of appropriate adjectives, powerful verbs and more especially adverbs, but through the feelings of the characters in the incidents in the still images. Much more emphasis on a higher vocabulary to emphasise the emotions of the participants.
- **Plenary – still image/thought tap:** Photo album plus the emotions of Lalchlan and Lila as each photograph appears. Ends with the same dialogue and then a discussion of the words used in the 'thoughts' part.

Lesson Four

W4

S3, 4

T13

- Time: 1 hour ten minutes
- **Text – teacher & class read:** Read letter left by Lila to her father as shared text. Discuss the manner and reason for its writing. Discuss how it should be read. What adverb would describe how to read it best?
- **Collective voice and mime:** Teacher in the role of Lila mimes writing the letter while the whole class takes on the role of the voice of Lila reading it aloud. This may take some rehearsals but will involve the children in the situation.
- **Conversations in pairs:** In pairs try out the argument between father and daughter leading to Lila's angry letter ending, 'Your ex-daughter'. What did Lalchlan say? What did Lila say? Discuss which words will be especially important in arguing out their case: e.g. but, if, then, on the other hand, so, etc.
- **Corporate voice:** One half of the class takes on the role of Lalchlan and the other half takes on the role of Lila. Two empty chairs opposite each other represent the two characters and the children take turns to continue the dia-

logue. Discuss how the argument went. Who 'won' if anyone? How do they think the characters felt by the end.

* **Forum theatre:** Two volunteers at a time come forward to play out the scene between Lalchlan and Lila. Others coming in and take on the roles, trying out changes that could possibly bring about a satisfying resolution to the dilemma between father and daughter. There will be continual discussion within this convention on how things are said, showing how subtext is linked so well with powerful adjectives, verbs and adverbs.

* **Independent and guided group work:** Independent work is collaborative writing of the above scene as they see it turning out. The guided group work is Group C looking at powerful adjectives and verbs to describe the mood and adverbs that describe how the various 'characters' behaved.

* **Plenary – performance or radio play:** Scripts in straight performance or as a radio play. Spellings recorded on board and practised.

Lesson Five

S4
T5

* **Time:** 1 hour
* **Children reading and performance (volunteered):** Children read the prepared script from the book. Teacher asks which they think is best and why. 'Is it because there is more emotion in yours?' Children work as actors with the book version.
* **Rehearsal/independent and guided work – scriptwriting:** The children rehearse the prepared script noting adverbs of how they perform the lines on the scripts. For example, Lila: 'Of course I do! (excitedly) It's the only thing I ever wanted' (longingly). Teacher works with one group to help on this.
* **Plenary – script performance:** Volunteer groups perform the script and give their adverb notes to the others so that they can discuss whether they succeeded in following their adverbial instructions.

A Highwayman Comes Riding
·using·
The Highwayman by Alfred Noyes

Michael Flemming is a Senior Lecturer in the School of Education, University of Durham where he is involved in graduate and undergraduate teacher training in Drama. Thanks are due to Mrs Scott and her Year 5 pupils at St Margaret's School, Durham City. His publications include The Art of Drama Teaching and Starting Drama Teaching.

This project was taught to a Year 5 class at St Margaret's Primary School in Durham City over a period of several weeks. By agreement with the class teacher the drama lessons did not replace the Literacy Hours for which the class were already scheduled. The project therefore concentrated more on trying out the drama activities rather than the specific literacy content. There are therefore two alternative approaches to using the ideas in this chapter. One would be for teachers to integrate the drama activities into the Literacy Hour as outlined here in the description of the project. Each lesson contains whole class text, sentence or word work, group/independent work and reviewing and reflection in accordance with the recommended structure for the Literacy Hour. The other approach would be to teach the drama lessons based on the stimulus material (perhaps during an afternoon) and use these as the basis for a separate Literacy Hour (the following morning). The advantage of this second approach is that the drama can have its own momentum and create motivation and understanding which feeds into the focused literacy work.

The project as described here seeks to integrate the drama with the word, sentence and text level work from the literacy framework. The objectives are drawn largely from Year 5 Term 2 so that teachers can incorporate the scheme more easily into their planning but some other additional objectives are included where these seem appropriate. Each lesson is intended to last a full hour. Considerable pace will be needed to include all the work particularly if the drama, as is often the case, takes on a momentum of its own. When teaching the lessons it may be necessary to be selective when setting the tasks unless the drama content is taught separately.

The Project

This project uses the narrative poem *The Highwayman* by Alfred Noyes for a series of drama/literacy activities with Year 5. The poem has been chosen because it is a popular text in schools and provides rich material for the Literacy Hour. Although it has been used in other published schemes its potential for drama has not been fully exploited and the ideas suggested here could be used to supplement other approaches. The introductory lesson seeks to use the strong narrative element in the poem by reading it in sections and predicting outcomes. The scheme as a whole is structured so that the pupils become familiar with the language and content of the poem before they begin to analyse the poetic effects more closely.

When reading the novel *Angela's Ashes* by Frank McCourt I was struck by a scene which describes the young Frank's naïve but authentic response to *The Highwayman*. A verse is recited to him each day while he is in hospital by a young girl, Patricia, who dies before she reaches the end of the poem:

> Every day I can't wait for the doctors and nurses to leave me alone so I can learn a new verse from Patricia and find out what's happening to the high-wayman and the landlord's red-lipped daughter. I love the poem because it is exciting. The redcoats are after the highwayman because they know he told her, 'I'll come to thee by moonlight, though hell should bar the way'.

The poem is often used in schools as a vehicle for teaching about poetic form without giving pupils an opportunity to enjoy its narrative and dramatic content. A common approach is for the class to read the poem through once and then set about identifying examples of particular rhythms and literary devices (for example onomatopoeia and metaphor) without any real appreciation of how content and form relate to create meaning. This tension is at the heart of teaching the Literacy Hour because it is easy to lose sight of overall meaning and enjoyment of texts in the pursuit of specific narrow objectives. It is all too easy for the Literacy Hour to become tedious and mechanical even though this was not the intention of the recommendations in the National Literacy Strategy. Here it is recognised that teachers should aim for 'high levels of motivation and active engagement of pupils' (DFEE: 8). Literacy instruction need not and should not be a substitute for enjoyment of language and engagement with themes in literary and other texts.

A major challenge facing teachers who are charged with implementing the Literacy Hour is how to maintain a balance between fulfilling specific language objectives and promoting the kind of genuine response to text which is a mark of good teaching. The goal is to promote what could be described as an 'integrated' approach to teaching which seeks to keep in balance content and form. This is not a new concern because it is the same challenge which effective teachers of poetry have had to meet. In the past ten years there has been increasing emphasis on the teacher's role in helping pupils make their own subjective responses to texts rather than simply concentrate on an 'objective' analysis of meaning and language. The change of emphasis was summarised by Benton et al (1988) as being a move from 'comprehension and criticism' to 'reading and response'. Similarly Dias and Hayhoe (1988) emphasised the constitutive (meaning making) role of the reader.

For pupils to engage with poetry (even more than other genres of writing) they need to be given time to respond to its content and enter its emotional territory. Drama can help them to take an active approach to reading and responding to the text, engaging with the language, characters and plot. Only then will the specific work on form have a context which makes it fully meaningful for the pupils.

In devising this project therefore one of my over-riding aims was that pupils should respond in much the way that the young Frank does in the novel: that the language and imagery should resonate with them through sheer familiarity and that they should appreciate the excitement of the romantic narrative. There is considerable emphasis on returning to the actual words of the poem when pupils have engaged in any drama related to its content. The scheme has been deliberately structured so that the poem is read several times both in its entirety and in sections. When the lessons were being tried out this was not a problem – the more the pupils became familiar with the language of the poem the more they enjoyed its sounds and rhythm. The more specific literacy teaching objectives described below, will be realised in meaningful rather than mechanical ways, if subordinate to the over-arching aim of having the pupils enjoy the poem.

Learning Objectives

Word level

* spelling strategies – building up spelling by syllabic parts, using known prefixes, suffixes and common letter strings
* exploring onomatopoeia

* investigating metaphorical expressions and figures of speech

Sentence level

* to re-order simple sentences, noting the changes which are required in word order and verb forms and discuss the effects of the changes
* to understand how writing can be adapted for different audiences and purposes, e.g. by changing vocabulary and sentence structures
* to be aware of the differences between spoken and written language
* use of first and third person pronouns

Text level

* to read a narrative poem
* to perform the poem; to understand terms which describe different kinds of poems
* to understand the difference between literal and figurative language
* to convert personal notes into notes for others to read
* to explore the use and effects of rhyme rhythm in poetry

Assessment

Opportunities for assessment arise not only through pupils' written work and oral responses in discussion but also through the specific drama activities which will reveal a considerable amount about pupils' understanding of content and form.

Lesson One

Lesson One focuses on the three characters and the language used to depict them. The children are encouraged to use prediction based on their growing knowledge of the characters.

The first thing I did was to write the word 'HIGHWAYMAN' on the board and ask the pupils to say what they understand by the term. I told them that they were going to read the first part of a poem which tells a story about a highwayman and they would be asked to guess what happens. I found it useful to include some historical background at this point, and told the children the following facts:

* highwaymen were common in Georgian England particularly in the 18th

century when the horse and carriage was a major source of transport for the rich

* highwaymen worked primarily on the major roads between cities
* if caught they received stiff penalties – usually death by hanging, sometimes transportation
* highwaymen tended not to kill their victims because they were able to escape easily on horseback over the open countryside.

I then read aloud Part One of the poem, emphasising in particular, the strong rhythm.

Part One

The wind was a torrent of darkness among the gusty trees,
The moon was a ghostly galleon tossed upon cloudy seas,
The road was a ribbon of moonlight over the purple moor,
And the highwayman came riding—
   Riding— riding—
The highwayman came riding up to the old inn-door.

He'd a French cocked-hat on his forehead, a bunch of lace at his chin,
A coat of the claret velvet, and breeches of brown doeskin:
They fitted with never a wrinkle; his boots were up to the thigh!
And he rode with a jewelled twinkle,
   His pistol butts a-twinkle,
His rapier hilt a-twinkle, under the jewelled sky.

Over the cobbles he clattered and clashed in the dark inn-yard,
And he tapped with his whip on the shutters, but all was locked and barred:
He whistled a tune to the window; and who should be waiting there
But the landlord's black-eyed daughter,
   Bess, the landlord's daughter,
Plaiting a dark red love-knot into her long black hair.

And dark in the dark old inn-yard a stable-wicket creaked
Where Tim, the ostler, listened; his face was white and peaked,
His eyes were hollows of madness, his hair like mouldy hay;
But he loved the landlord's daughter,
   The landlord's red-lipped daughter:
Dumb as a dog he listened, and he heard the robber say—

"One kiss, my bonny sweet heart, I'm after a prize tonight,

But I shall be back with the yellow gold before the morning light.
Yet if they press me sharply, and harry me through the day,
Then look for me by moonlight,
    Watch for me by moonlight:
I'll come to thee by moonlight, though Hell should bar the way."

He rose upright in the stirrups, he scarce could reach her hand;
But she loosened her hair i' the casement! His face burnt like a brand
As the black cascade of perfume came tumbling over his breast;
And he kissed its waves in the moonlight,
    (Oh, sweet black waves in the moonlight)
Then he tugged at his reins in the moonlight, and galloped away to the West.

The pupils were then asked to read Part One again, and work out how many characters there are in this part of the poem, who they are and what we are told about each one. This is not a straightforward task for the pupils – they need to establish that there are *three* characters (The highwayman, Tim the ostler and Bess the landlord's daughter). Explain any word which they do not understand: e.g. ostler (stableman), peaked (sickly), wicket (gate), press/harry (harass or chase), casement (window), priming (preparing muskets for fire).

In order to elicit an initial response to this section of the poem and to make sure the class have understood its content, I asked the following questions:

1 How do we know the events are set in the past?
2 Can we guess anything about each character that we are not told in the poem?
3 Which character is likely to be the hero? (This may lead to a focus on the words or imagery used to describe the highwayman and the ostler).
4 Establish clearly that both the ostler and the highwayman love Bess.

Group writing

I divided the class into groups and asked each group to write words or phrases from the verses about the physical appearance of each character onto character templates (figures drawn in outline so that pupils can write inside them). For example:

Highwayman: French cocked-hat; lace at his chin; velvet coat; doeskin
                    breeches; high boots.

Ostler: white, peaked face; hollow eyes; hair like mouldy hay.
Bess: black-eyed, long black hair, red-lipped, hair black waves.

The pupils were then asked to look at their lists and identify which of the words are nouns and which adjectives. As a class, we then discussed what the descriptions told us about the characters.

We then looked at the spelling of the word 'highwayman', written on the board, and I drew the pupils' attention to the syllables, and the fact that the word is actually made up of three words – 'high', 'way' and 'man'. We then related this back to the meaning of the word – someone who robbed people on highways. I told the pupils that breaking a word down in this way is sometimes a useful way of remembering how to spell it, and asked them as a group to identify other words in this part of the poem which contain words inside them (either two words as with 'landlord', 'sweetheart', 'moonlight' or one word plus suffix as in 'jewelled'). We then as a group tried to think of other words which contain words within them.

Still images

I asked for volunteers in the class to describe the life they imagine the three characters identified might have led (ostler working in the stable, Bess working in the inn, highwayman on the roads). The children worked in small groups to prepare three images depicting an everyday scene each involving one of the three characters. I asked the groups to present their images in such a way that the rest of the class could guess which character was being depicted. The purpose here is to establish the context of the poem and to introduce the creation of still images through a straightforward activity. I presented it as a challenge to the pupils that they should be able to keep absolutely still and silent when others in the class were looking at the image. It is a good idea for the pupils to practice the technique when creating still images which are not too difficult in terms of content.

Thought tracking

Having performed the still imaging task, the groups were asked to devise a still image which involved the three characters together. Volunteers showed the images and as they do so read any relevant lines from the poem. For example:

And dark in the dark old inn-yard a stable-wicket creaked
Where Tim, the ostler, listened; his face was white and peaked . . .

He whistled a tune to the window; and who should be waiting there
But the landlord's black-eyed daughter . . .

As the class watched and responded to the images, I asked further speculative questions:

1 Does Bess know that the ostler loves her?
2 Does the landlord know that Bess is seeing the highwayman?
3 We are not told anything about Bess's mother – what might have happened to her?
4 What does the ostler think of the highwayman?
5 How does the highwayman treat the ostler?

Each group now repeated the image involving all three characters, but this time including the thoughts of each of them which are voiced in turn. Again, it may be possible to integrate actual words from the poem.

Conclusion

The pupils were asked to make inferences about how the poem might continue – what have we learned about the characters?; what are we *not* told in this part of the poem that we might like to know?; what do they think will happen in the rest of the poem?

To conclude the session, the pupils were asked to write an entry of a diary in role as either the ostler, Bess or the highwayman. We discussed the difference between writing in the third and first person. The diaries could deal with the events in the first section of the poem or the pupils could use the diary to indicate how they think the narrative might develop. I asked them to pay particular attention to the spelling of key words and reminded them of the techniques they learned earlier to remember spellings.

Lesson Two

Lesson Two began with a recap on what the pupils remembered about the poem. We read some of the diary extracts from lesson one, then speculated again on what might happen. I explained that the term 'narrative poem' refers to a poem like this which tells a story. Several of the pupils in the class had actually been to the library between the two lessons to find the poem to see how it continued! Now the whole class would be involved in presenting a reading of the poem and trying to create an appropriate atmosphere.

Teacher reading

The whole poem was read, including Part One from the previous lesson.

Part Two

He did not come in the dawning; he did not come at noon;
And out of the tawny sunset, before the rise o' the moon,
When the road was a gipsy's ribbon, looping the purple moor,
A red-coat troop came marching—
    Marching— marching—
King George's men came marching, up to the old inn-door.

They said no word to the landlord, they drank his ale instead;
But they gagged his daughter and bound her to the foot of her narrow bed.
Two of them knelt at her casement, with muskets at the side!
There was death at every window;
    And Hell at one dark window;
But Bess could see, through her casement, the road that he would ride.

They had tied her up to attention, with many a sniggering jest:
They had bound a musket beside her, with the barrel beneath her breast!
"Now keep good watch!" and they kissed her.
    She heard the dead man say—
Look for me by moonlight;
Watch for me by moonlight;
I'll come to thee by moonlight, though Hell should bar the way!

She twisted her hands behind her; but all the knots held good!
She writhed her hands till her fingers were wet with sweat or blood!
They stretched and strained in the darkness, and the hours crawled by like years;
Till now, on the stroke of midnight,
    Cold, on the stroke of midnight,
The tip of one finger touched it! The trigger at least was hers!

The tip of one finger touched it; she strove no more for the rest!
Up, she stood up to attention, with the barrel beneath her breast,
She would not risk their hearing; she would not strive again;
For the road lay bare in the moonlight,
    Blank and bare in the moonlight;
And the blood of her veins in the moonlight throbbed to her Love's refrain.

Tlot-tlot, tlot-tlot! Had they heard it? The horse-hoofs ringing clear—

Tlot-tlot, tlot-tlot, in the distance? Were they deaf that they did not hear?
Down the ribbon of moonlight, over the brow of the hill,
The highwayman came riding,
    Riding, riding!
The red-coats looked to their priming! She stood up straight and still!

Tlot-tlot in the frosty silence! Tlot-tlot in the echoing night!
Nearer he came and nearer! Her face was like a light!
Her eyes grew wide for a moment; she drew one last deep breath,
Then her fingers moved in the moonlight,
    Her musket shattered the moonlight,
Shattered her breast in the moonlight and warned him – with her death.

He turned; he spurred him westward; he did not know who stood
Bowed with her head o'er the musket, drenched with her own red blood!
Not till the dawn he heard it, and slowly blanched to hear
How Bess, the landlord's daughter,
    The landlord's black-eyed daughter,
Had watched for her love in the moonlight; and died in the darkness there.

Back, he spurred like a madman, shrieking a curse to the sky,
With the white road smoking behind him, and his rapier brandished high!
Blood-red were his spurs in the golden noon; wine-red was his velvet coat;
When they shot him down on the highway,
Down like a dog on the highway,
And he lay in his blood on the highway, with the bunch of lace at his throat.

And still of a winter's night, they say, when the wind is in the trees,
When the moon is a ghostly galleon tossed upon the cloudy seas,
When the road is a ribbon of moonlight over the purple moor,
A highwayman comes riding—
    Riding— Riding—
A highwayman comes riding, up to the old inn-door.

Over the cobbles he clatters and clangs in the dark inn-yard;
And he taps with his whip on the shutters, but all is locked and barred:
He whistles a tune to the window, and who should be waiting there
But the landlord's black-eyed daughter,
    Bess, the landlord's daughter,
Plaiting a dark red love-knot into her long black hair.

I established that the pupils understood what has happened but did not focus on the poetic effects at this stage. Many of these will be implicitly discovered by the pupils themselves through their performance of the poem.

Word and sentence work

I explained to the pupils that the whole class would be performing the poem and that the work in the next part of the lesson would help them to do that well. This gave them a purpose which would interest them, and re-engage them with the poem.

In small groups, the pupils picked out any words related to sounds in the poem. We examined the grammar of these words – which are verbs, etc. I introduced the term 'onomatopoeia' in relation to the sound of the hooves' 'tlot-tlot'. I asked the pupils to think of other such words for the sound of a musket firing, the sound of a window shutting, etc.

The groups then identified the direct speech in the poem. I first made sure that the pupils understood the difference between direct and indirect speech. We discussed why speech marks are used for some words spoken, but italics for others.

Soundtracking

In order to engage the pupils more effectively, I involved them in discussion of how the poem should be read and presented using mime, still images and sound effects. We decided to use different voices for the different characters' direct speech, and to include some choral reading. Some of the verses could be read by groups, others by individuals. We discussed pace – speeding up the reading as the sound of the horse comes closer in the second section, etc. We decided to limit mime to moments when the soldiers wait in the inn and on the highway, as miming the entire poem would become too complex.

We concluded that sound effects would be best inserted after a pause at the beginning or end of a line rather than at the same time as the spoken words. The marching feet of the soldiers is effective if the noise builds to a crescendo and then a sudden halt; the sound of the horse on the cobbles (two upturned lids or plastic cups) is likewise effective if it fades in during the reading and rises to a crescendo.

Performance and discussion

Having rehearsed their particular contribution in small groups, the class as a whole rehearsed and performed a polished version. I drew attention to the way in which the pupils responded to the rhythm and rhyme of the poem as they were reading it. I then asked them to identify the rhyme which is the same for each verse (aabccb) and rhythmic patterns, and to identify any examples of repetition in the poem. We then consolidated our work on onomatopoeia, and closed the lesson.

Lesson Three

The focus in the drama in this lesson was on the characters other than Bess and the highwayman – the ostler, the landlord and the soldiers. We first recapped on what has happened in the poem. We then embarked on a discussion of the character of the ostler. What might have happened between the first and second part of the poem? If the pupils had the chance to question the ostler what would they ask him?

Teacher in role

I explained to the pupils that whenever I put on my hat, I was in the role of the ostler, and when I removed the hat, the role play was over. In role, I invited the students to question me, assuming that it was now some weeks after the events of the poem. The class sustained this part of the lesson for an extraordinary length of time including questions such as:

'Did you tell the soldiers that the highwayman would be coming back to the inn?'
'When and how did you sneak out of the inn?'
'Did you expect the highwayman to die?'
'Why didn't you help Bess when the soldiers came?'
'How long have you worked at the inn?'
'Was Bess kind to you?'
'What did you think of the highwayman?'

I found that it was not necessary for the teacher to place a strong emphasis on acting the part – it was enough to adopt an attitude in answering the questions. The pupils can be prompted to ask more complex questions by the teacher's answers or can be reminded of some of the lines of the poem. For example:

Question: How long have you worked at the inn?
Ostler: Much too long if you want to know – five or six years.

Question: Did you tell the soldiers about the highwayman?
Ostler: Look I hope you're not blaming me for their deaths – I never wanted them dead, particularly Bess.

Question: What did you think of the highwayman?
Ostler: To be honest I didn't like him. He thought a lot of himself with his French cocked hat and all that lace. He really thought he was something in his velvet coat. What chance did I have with Bess?

Question: Did you listen to the highwayman talking to Bess?
Ostler: Not deliberately. I was just finishing my work. I had just shut the stable wicket and I heard what sounded like a whistle. I stopped and listened. It was dark in the inn yard and I couldn't see very well but I heard a voice say something like 'my bonny sweetheart'. That made me listen even more closely if you want to know.

Hotseating

Volunteers from the class can now try being the ostler or take the role of other characters to be questioned. These do not have to be characters who actually appear in the poem and might include the landlord, the commanding officer of the soldiers or someone who was drinking at the inn when the soldiers came. I found it useful to encourage the pupils to speculate and range outside the frame of reference of the poem (e.g. how Bess got on with her father; did he know what was going on?). If several versions of the ostler are presented the pupils can be asked to say which version matches the character as he is presented in the poem.

I introduced the term 'imagery' at this point, and referred the pupils back to the work on the description of the characters in Lesson Two – the way in which we receive an impression of the characters from the way they are described.

Word level work

I explained that the atmosphere of the poem is also created by the visual images – the pictures conjured up in our minds. Many of these are metaphors – when something is described as something else in order to make a comparison (e.g. the moon was a ghostly galleon tossed upon cloudy seas; the road was a ribbon of moonlight; sweet black waves in the moonlight). In groups, the pupils were asked to identify other images in the poem and to explain their purpose, for example, the moon was probably a crescent shape and is being compared to a ship floating on the waves of the sea. The pupils then listed any metaphors they found in the poem. To conclude the lesson, we reinforced the way the descriptions of the characters, the images and metaphors all contributed to the atmosphere of the poem.

Lesson Four

After briefly recapping on the content of the poem, this lesson concentrated on what happened at the inn. We imagined a scenario where although the soldiers were proud of the fact that they had ambushed and killed the highwayman, they kept quiet about what happened to Bess. A week or so after the events described in the poem, the commanding officer has sent two investigators back to the inn in order to find out what had happened to Bess. At this stage I introduced the historical fact that highwaymen often used coaching inns as a refuge when they were being pursued. They often bribed the innkeeper to keep quiet about their presence. There have been some examples of wealthy and well known people who became highwaymen when they ran into debt. They frequently wore masks so they could not be identified.

Pairs demonstration

I invited one of the pupils to take the part of the landlord who is questioned by the teacher in role as an investigator. The purpose of the demonstration is to help the pupils enact their own scenes. I encouraged the pupils to think of such things as: what is the landlord doing when the knock comes on the door?; does he welcome the investigator in straightaway or is he reluctant at first? I paused occasionally to ask the pupils to suggest possible questions and ideas for conducting the investigation. Some questions we came up with were:

> I realise you must still be distressed at the death of your daughter, but do you mind answering some questions we would like to put to you?
> What mood were the soldiers in when they arrived at the inn?
> Could you show me exactly where they sat?
> Did you overhear any of their conversations?
> You say you remained upstairs in your room when the soldier arrived – did you hear anything unusual?
> Could we go to the room in which Bess's body was found?
> You say that Bess spent quite a lot of time with the highwayman – could you tell me more about that please?
> You say you left the inn before the soldiers and came back to find Bess dead. Were you not worried leaving her like that?

I pointed out to the pupils that more interest and tension is created if the land-lord is either concealing what happened or for some reason does not know himself. The same applies to the other characters who might be interviewed: people who were drinking in the inn that evening, the ostler, one of the soldiers. We discussed the difficulties of taking notes while interviewing – it is important not to stop the flow of the questions and answers, but key points needed to be noted so they could be remembered. When might it be necessary to write down someone's exact words?

Small group work

We organised into groups of four or five to act out the investigations. These do not just have to involve question and answer interviews but might involve varied actions for example, the investigators can be shown to various rooms which are critical to the investigation or they might search the inn. Pupils should be given some assistance with this drama work which they may find difficult.

The pupils then worked out exactly how the scene would begin and end, and I encouraged them to think of appropriate actions during the interviews. The investigators were told to take notes as they conducted their investigations – as well as being part of the written exercise, this served as a helpful prop for the acting.

Writing

I encouraged the pupils to write a report for the commanding officer saying what they think has happened and what their evidence is. I drew their attention to the fact that the commanding officer was not there so he would need to be supplied with details of the context. This is a challenging writing exercise but one towards which the pupils will be motivated if their drama has gone well. It might help them to be given a layout and headings for their report, for example, purpose of investigation, incident being investigated, people interviewed, the investigation, conclusions. Alternatively, it might be helpful to give them the first section of the report, depending on their ability.

Lesson Five

The final lesson focused on examining the events of the poem from a modern day perspective. We first re-read the final two verses of the poem. It is now in the present day and the inn is still used as a pub and guest house. I asked the pupils to imagine how the inn might have changed, and to establish a name for it (e.g. 'The Boar's Head'). Why do the manager and some of the guests think that the place is haunted? What have they heard or seen?

Television programme

The pupils then enacted a modern day television programme, with guests and an invited participating audience, which looks into reportings of strange happenings. The pupils were asked to think of a name for the programme for example, 'Face the Facts', 'Into the Unknown' or 'Would You Believe It?' The subject of the programme is the supposed haunting at the inn.

I found that the best way to explain to the pupils what is required was to do this through active drama. After a minimum of explanation I adopted the role of the presenter of the show and proceeded to interview members of the invited audience (the pupils). An example of an introductory 'script' is given below:

> Good evening ladies and gentlemen and welcome to another edition of 'Face the Facts'.
> Tonight on our show we hear about the strange goings on at the The Boar's Head here in Gloucester. Amongst our audience we have the manager and several of his staff plus many guests who have spent a night at the inn and have strange tales to report. I believe sir [*the teacher with an imaginary microphone turns to one of the pupils*] that you spent a night at the inn several weeks ago. Could you tell us what you heard during the night that kept you awake?

The pupils very quickly caught on to the convention and I paused to appoint some pupils to specific roles, e.g. people who have spent a night at the inn, one or two sceptics in the studio who are not convinced by the explanations. It is a good idea to discuss with the pupils how more tension can be created by having ambiguous and circumstantial evidence presented first of all rather than a full citing of any ghostly apparition.

During this lesson one of the pupils was asked what the weather was like when he stayed at the inn and he replied, without reference to the text and without any hint of irony: 'It was very windy. The moon was like a ghostly galleon in the sky'. It was a rewarding moment that the language of the poem had become so familiar to him without any conscious effort. It did, however, suggest a possible focus for some of the literacy work: exploring the way in which language changes according to different genres and contexts. If pupils integrate actual words from the poem into the television programme the incongruity creates a humorous effect and makes precisely the point about appropriateness of language in a very graphic way.

Small group

I asked pupils in small groups to go though the poem and make a list of phrases or sentences in one column and in another column write an alternative word order.

Over the cobbles he clattered and clashed	He clattered and clashed over the cobbles.
He tapped with his whip on the shutters.	He tapped on the shutters with his whip.
Down the ribbon of moonlight ...	The highwayman came riding
The highwayman came riding	down the river of moonlight
Not till the dawn he heard it.	He heard it not till the dawn.

We then discussed the reasons why certain word order is preferable in the poem (for the purposes of rhyme, for emphasis), and how conventions about word order change over time.

We then returned to the drama. I told the pupils that after the television programme a discovery was made at the inn which provided an account of what might have happened there all those years ago: the poem itself. The pupils suggested that a diary of one of the characters had been found. This provides another opportunity to explore different writing conventions between poem and diary.

The pupils' final task was to prepare in small groups a reconstruction (in still image form or small group enactment) for the next television programme of one of the events suggested by the poem. Pupils needed to be guided towards tasks which were manageable for them. For example it would not be appropriate for them to try to act out all the events which happened when the soldiers arrived at the inn. They could, however, easily present the scene which took place when the soldiers were ordering their drinks. Some groups needed to be directed towards still images.

The task here is quite challenging but that is appropriate for the culmination of the work. The project has been structured so that there is a steady progression over the five lessons in both level of difficulty of the literacy work and in the drama content.

Bibliography

Benton, M., Teasy, J., Bell, R. & Hurst, K., *Young Readers Responding to Poems*, Routledge, 1988.

Dias, P. & Hayhoe, M. *Developing Response to Poetry*, Open University Press, 1988.

Useful resources

An edition of *The Highwayman* published by Oxford University Press contains some very striking illustrations by Charles Keeping.

For historical background see Michael Billett, *Highwaymen and Outlaws*, Arms and Armour Press, 1997, which has a good bibliography.

Loreena McKennit has put *The Highwayman* to music on the CD *The Book of Secrets.*

Lesson Guide

Literacy learning

Word level

Revision of nouns and adjectives; using independent spelling strategies – building up spellings by syllabic parts; onomatopoeia; agreement between nouns and verbs; direct speech.

Sentence level

Note making; to convert personal notes into notes for others to read; to re-order simple sentences, noting the changes which are required in word order and verb forms, and discuss the effects of the changes.

Text level

To investigate metaphorical expression; literal and figurative language.

Resources

Copies of The *Highwayman*, plain white paper, character templates (figures drawn in outline so that pupils can write inside them), pens, miscellaneous objects to use for sound effects (upturned cups, triangle for strokes of midnight), a hat or scarf to symbolise when the teacher is in role, an object to use as an imaginary microphone.

Lesson One

Year 5 • Term 2
W3, W8
S4
T4, T5

* **Role on the wall:** Write the word 'HIGHWAYMAN' on the board – discuss the word.
* **Teacher reading:** Read Part One of the poem, emphasising strong rhythm.
* **Pupil response:** Pupils to work out characters and their motivations.
* **Group writing:** Using character templates, write words and phrases from the poem about physical appearance of characters.
* **Still images:** Small groups create still images depicting everyday scenes in life of characters. Rest of class to guess who they are portraying. Then still image of all three characters together.
* **Conclusion:** How might poem continue? What have we learned about characters? Diary entry in role.

Lesson Two

W 11
S2, S6
T5

* **Teacher reading:** Read whole poem.
* **Word and sentence work:** Small groups to pick out onomatopoeic words in poem, and examine grammar. Same groups to identify direct speech in poem.
* **Soundtracking:** Suggestions for presentation of performance of poem – mime, still images, sound effects, different voices for direct speech.
* **Performance and discussion:** Class as a whole rehearse and perform a polished version. Consolidate work on onomatopoeia.

Lesson Three

W12
T10

* **Teacher in role:** Teacher in role as the Ostler, class to interview.
* **Hotseating:** Volunteers take on role of a character and are questioned by rest of class.
* **Word level work:** Explain how atmosphere created by visual images – metaphors etc.

Lesson Four

* **Pairs demonstration:** One pupil is inn landlord, questioned by teacher in role as investigator. Then in pairs, pupils enact their own investigations.
* **Small group work:** Work out entire scene of investigator at inn. Take notes during investigations.
* **Writing:** Pupils to write report for commanding officer saying what happened, and provide supporting evidence.

T21, S2

Lesson Five

* **Television programme:** Pupils to act out modern day TV programme looking into reports of strange happenings. Subject is haunting at the inn.
* **Small group work:** Pupils to create alternative word order for phrases from poem. After TV documentary, poem is discovered – pupils to construct follow-up TV programme involving still images, acting out events etc.

S1, S3

'A Special Kind of Freedom', The Oral Tradition and Dramatic Composition
·using·
the West Indian stories of *Anancy-Spiderman*

Helen Nicholson is a lecturer in the School of Education, Homerton College, Cambridge. Helen has co-ordinated and co-authored The Secondary Teacher's Handbook, *a new National Drama publication.*

The work I am about to describe, based on the West Indian stories of Anancy, has been undertaken, appropriately, in more than one context. I say 'appropriately' because at the heart of this drama lies the oral tradition of storytelling, a tradition which takes account of the contemporary, the new and the unforeseen, adapts to its audience, and yet uses forms, structures and characters which remain recognisable and familiar.

The Anancy-Spiderman project took place with two Year 5 classes in different schools, whose interpretation of the Literacy Strategy varied. I made weekly visits to one large primary school, where the staff recognised that their literacy policies were already strong. They had made the decision to integrate the National Literacy Strategy into all their teaching, but not to introduce a particular Literacy Hour. In the other school, there was a more literal interpretation of the document; the children spent an hour each day working within the recommended framework, and it was not proving very popular. I was invited to the school for four consecutive days, to work intensively with a Year 5 class. My intention was not to use drama to liven up the curriculum, although I certainly hoped that the children would enjoy the experience. Rather, I planned a structure which was primarily aimed at encouraging the children to engage creatively in drama and, by focusing on elements of dramatic composition, to develop their literacy skills. In writing this chapter, I have drawn particularly on my work with this class.

The Anancy-Spiderman Project

In choosing Anancy stories for the project, I was responding to The National Literacy Strategy, which identifies traditional tales from a range of cultures as suitable texts for Year 5 pupils. However, I was also interested in the dramatic potential of the Anancy stories. Anancy, the hero of many West Indian folk tales, is a trickster; the landscape he inhabits, his exploits, the characters he meets and the fact that the stories are bound up in the history of slavery combine to provide rich and multi-layered texts which invite re-interpretation in dramatic form. Indeed, as a character from the oral tradition, Anancy's stories have been told in many ways, in different contexts, and have changed over time. For drama, and its relationship to literacy learning, the oral tradition provides children with a particular opportunity to adapt, reinvent and re-tell the stories for themselves.

There were two main educational principles which guided the work, and which became increasingly inter-related as the project progressed. Firstly, I wanted to explore the stories *as* drama, and to explore the roles, structures and dramatic devices intrinsic to the stories themselves. Secondly, I was interested in the different ways in which children learn, and intended to provide a structure which included a range of learning styles. Current research into learning styles suggests that children learn differently. Some are primarily visual learners, preferring the written word, diagrams, pictures and other visual images; some are mainly auditory learners, who find it easier to learn through talk, discussion and listening to others, and some children, perhaps the most neglected by traditional teaching methods, are kinaesthetic learners, who remember what they do and experience, who work through problems physically and, crucially for a literacy strategy, are often poor spellers. If this is the case, in order for all children to be included in the work, I needed to vary the learning styles, to provide children with different points of entry into the drama, and different ways of combining learning styles to improve their standards of literacy. Furthermore, as many experienced learners use a range of strategies, I also wanted to extend children's repertoire of learning styles, and to offer them support in aspects of the work they found more difficult.

It is interesting that drama almost always includes a range of learning styles within the form itself. More literal interpretations of the Literacy Hour, and those which do not include drama, are unlikely to reach kinaesthetic learners, who may well be the very children who experience literacy difficulties. Drama, which is a kinaesthetic, visual and aural art form, can make a significant contribution to children's literacy learning because it is so multi-modal. It is because drama combines the different 'modes' of space, movement, words, image, sound and so on, that it enables children to find different ways of developing the necessary conceptual and intellectual understanding to communicate in language. Indeed, in a multi-media age, it has long been argued that literacy includes more than the written word.

The text which I used most extensively in this project was James Berry's re-telling of the Anancy stories, in a book called *Anancy-Spiderman*. Berry's introduction to the book identifies the relationship between the written text and the oral tradition, where he acknowledges that he has both drawn on his experiences of hearing the stories during his Caribbean childhood and that, in writing them down, he has 'deepened, clarified and expanded the stories'. His stories include information about the characters and situations which might be missed out when they are told to an audience who share the same tradition of story telling. In specifically dramatic terms, Berry acknowledges that 'an expanded staging' enables the stories to travel, and reach new audiences. This seemed particularly appropriate for the project with Year 5 pupils; many had not heard the stories before, although some children were already familiar with Anancy and this gave them a particular sense of pride and ownership of the work.

In terms of literacy, the Anancy-Spiderman stories offer much on the basis of text level work. During the course of the project, the children became familiar with the features and structure of the genre, the differences between oral and written story telling, the way in which stories had changed over time and how, as an author, James Berry acknowledged his sources. They investigated the viewpoints of different characters in a highly practical way and prepared notes to help them tell their own stories. However, it was also the wealth of dramatic devices contained in the stories which particularly drew me to them. The roles of the trickster and the accomplice, the use of disguise and deception, the reversal of fortune and the final pay-off enabled me to teach the children about dramatic structures and forms. And, as in all good traditional tales, there is a moral dimension to the stories which invites dialogue, discussion and debate.

The project was divided into four separate lessons, each of which broadly followed the recommended structure of the Literacy Hour. Each lesson included all the elements of the Literacy Strategy – word, sentence and text level work – although the prescriptive time schedules were not always conducive to learning, and I sometimes found it necessary to adapt the order or balance of the hour. The work was designed to include a range of learning styles in every lesson. Over the course of the project, the children worked kinaesthetically on a poem; they used their aural and verbal skills to re-tell a story orally; they wrote short scripts for performance; they investigated the cultural context of the stories. The work thus included a range of different types of reading and writing, which included poetry, stories, playscripts, non-fiction texts and CD-ROM software.

Learning Objectives

The Anancy-Spiderman project was planned focusing on learning objectives associated with the exploration of text, and word and sentence level work was integrated into the project as whole. In this way aspects of literacy specifically concerned with spelling, vocabulary, grammar, sentence construction and punctuation were regarded in context, as intrinsic to textual readings and the children's own writing. The work included the following learning objectives:

Word level

* to keep individual lists of words and to learn to spell them
* to use antonyms to show the two sides of Anancy's character
* to explore onomatopoeia by making 'found poems'

Sentence level

* to understand how writing can be adapted for different audiences and purposes, particularly the audiences for plays and the purpose of the oral tradition of storytelling
* to be aware of the differences between spoken and written language, including the use of the conventions of stage directions to guide readers; the need for scripts to make sense for other performers; the use of punctuation to indicate intonation, pauses, gestures established in the rehearsal process

Text level

* to identify and classify the features of Anancy stories, such as structure, form and characterisation
* to recognise the cultural context of the stories and the place and setting expressed in Anancy stories
* to explore the differences between oral and written storytelling
* to perform poems in a variety of ways
* to investigate the narrative viewpoint and the viewpoints of different characters
* to substitute their own words to a poem about Anancy

* to write their own version of an Anancy story, using structures and themes identified in reading
* to make notes of story outline as preparation for oral storytelling
* to locate information about the slave-trade using information books and CD-ROM
* to consider how James Berry, as an author, records and acknowledges his sources

Assessment

The four-lesson project included a wide range of learning objectives and, in practice, it is impossible to assess every child on each. For assessment purposes, I decided to focus on particular areas of learning. I also wanted to communicate the assessment criteria to the children, which also helped me to keep the learning objectives in mind, and to reinforce particular aspects of learning as the project developed. The assessment criteria included three categories: word, sentence and text level work.

Word level

* can use spelling log to record new words, identifies adjectives and adverbs
* shows understanding of antonyms in describing character
* experiments with onomatopoeia in 'found' poems

Sentence level

* adapts writing for different audiences and purposes
* uses stage directions and punctuation to show intonation, gesture, pauses

Text level

* constructs own version of Anancy story, using knowledge of structure, form and characterisation
* shows understanding of differences between oral, written and dramatised stories
* performs poem using voice and movement
* able to write a dramatic script by substituting own words to a poem

Managing assessment is difficult, particularly in a tightly structured hour-long lesson in which I, as a teacher, was actively involved. In order to find opportunities to assess the children on the criteria I had identified, I needed to use a variety of methods. I tried to balance the assessment of written or recorded work with assessment of the children's oral contributions within the drama itself. For reasons which will become clear, I also provided opportunities for children to show their literacy learning creatively, in the drama itself, through the use of their voices and movement, in improvised dialogue, as storytellers, as well as in discussion and evaluative talk. I employed, therefore, a number of assessment methods, including visual and written work – scripts, notes, 'found poems', maps, spelling logs; oral and aural work – discussion, improvisation, intonation; kinaesthetic work – choreographed movement, gesture and facial expression.

Lesson One

Poetry, movement and character

The project began with a poem, rather than the story. Recognising that many would not have 'met' Anancy before, and mindful of James Berry's observation that in oral storytelling there is much information which is taken on trust, I wanted to ensure that the children had some prior knowledge of Anancy before we heard the stories. The poem I chose was Andrew Salkey's poem *Anancy*, which gives a visual image of Anancy. I laid out some props on the floor, a waistcoat, a cane, and a top hat and, telling the class that these belonged to the person in our drama, I asked for a volunteer to try them on. What kind of person was he? How would he walk? How do you have to stand to wear them? Having observed the child wearing the costume, the class experimented with walking around the room in ways which befitted Anancy's mode of dress. Following this, I asked them how it made them feel. They said they felt important, superior, clever and proud, as one boy put it, 'he is better than anyone else, or he thinks he is'. Armed with this insight, we read together the first two stanzas the poem, which immediately locate Anancy in his cultural context.

> Anancy is a spider;
> Anancy is a man;
> Anancy is West Indian
> And West African.
>
> Sometimes, he wears a waistcoat;
> Sometimes he carries a cane;
> Sometimes, he sports a top hat;
> Sometimes, he's just a plain,
> Ordinary, black, hairy, spider.

Andrew Salkey

So what could we add to our image of Anancy? Back on their feet, the children composed a simple movement piece. To the beat of an African drum, they travelled to four different areas of the room and at each point created a still image of Anancy. Taking the lines in turn, the children created an image of Anancy wearing a waistcoat, in the second and third places they added an imaginary cane and then top hat, and in the final place they became Anancy as a spider. Following a discussion of their individual work, I gave them extracts of the next part of the poem to work on in groups, where their task was to create a moving image which showed the characteristics of Anancy, and experiment with ways of vocalising the lines of the poem imaginatively. The group work was put together with the choreography of the first two stanzas and, having developed a quick movement piece to show Anancy returning to a spider in the final stanza of the poem, the class were able to give a collective performance of the poem.

The poem, when performed as a movement piece, was a particularly effective way of introducing the children to Anancy. They found, by working on the physical characteristics of the role, that Anancy has two sides to his personality. On a large piece of paper, we drew the shape of a man in a top-hat and they recorded on his body adverbs to describe his movement, and adjectives to describe his character. This provided an opportunity to focus on their visual skills as spellers, as well as consolidating their understanding of adverbs and adjectives. I then asked them, in pairs, to write down appropriate antonyms to describe how it felt to be Anancy as a spider. Because they had worked physically on the role, they were well aware of the differences in size and status between spiders and men (they had all worked at floor level when creating the movement of a spider), antonyms were varied and fairly easily found. However, they did not agree that Anancy's pride as a man was matched by humility as a spider. On the contrary, as a spider he had, as one girl put it, 'a special kind of freedom, not to behave like other people think he should'. The focus on the physicality of the role had enabled the children, with very little explanation from me, to find the symbolic importance of Anancy. With his history in the slave trade and in centuries of black oppression, they had discovered the heart of the stories. Anancy represents, in West Indian folklore, a very special kind of freedom.

Lesson Two

Telling the story

In the second lesson I chose to focus on James Berry's story, *Mrs Anancy,*

Chicken Soup and Anancy, which offers particular opportunities for drama and literacy learning. In terms of literacy, I wanted to encourage children to explore the structure of the folk-tale genre, to add to their knowledge of Anancy as a character, to select information from the story and to physicalise their findings in voice and movement. Drawing on genre theory, my aim was to encourage the children to become familiar with the structure and style of the folk-tale in order that they might use this understanding to identify and emphasise particular words, phrases, events and roles which characterise the genre.

I began by reading the story to the class. Having become acquainted with Anancy in the previous lesson, the children were keen to hear, as one child put it, 'what he got up to in his stories'. I was also keen to take every opportunity to explore the dramatic potential in the story. The plot of *Mrs Anancy, Chicken Soup and Anancy* follows a classic four act structure.

1 Anancy decides to trick his wife by faking illness because he wants to eat the chickens Mrs Anancy has been fattening up to sell. He enlists the help of his accomplice, Bro Dog.
2 Finding Anancy ill, Mrs Anancy leaves to fetch the doctor. Anancy tries to persuade her to take the long way round, although she becomes suspicious and follows him.
3 When she reaches the doctor's surgery she sees Anancy talking to Bro Dog. In disguise, Bro Dog tells her that the only thing that will cure Anancy is chicken soup. When Mrs Anancy arrives home, Anancy is singing. When she enters, he groans in pain.
4 Mrs Anancy, realising that Anancy is trying to trick her, visits her friend Dora to invite twenty-four children to a feast. She returns home, cooks the chicken, and the children eat it. Anancy's plans have been thwarted.

Following this structure, we divided the story into acts and scenes, each group taking responsibility for dramatising a particular section of the story. Their first task was to re-read their part of the story, and to summarise the action by drawing a map which charted the key events. This map was then used as the basis for a series of still images, to represent Anancy's journey.

Returning to the written text, they underlined all the words or phrases they especially liked. They experimented with onomatopoeic expressions such as 'fattened', 'tired groans', 'must hurry', 'terrible pain', 'tempting cooking' which they added to the still images, as 'found' poems, to create dramatic atmosphere. The lesson concluded with the children recording their favourite words in their spelling logs, identifying adjectives, verbs or adverbs, and reflecting on how the texture and sound of these words represented and created the different moods of the story.

This combination of the visual representation of ideas in words and pictures with sounds and movement both included a range of learning styles, and is central to drama and the oral tradition of storytelling. Indeed, James Berry's written text of *Mrs Anancy, Chicken Soup and Anancy* includes songs, and his use of repetition and colloquialisms implies a hearer, as well as a reader. As Bryant and Bradley (1985) demonstrated, enlarging the children's experience of literacy relies on them developing an understanding of language as it is heard, where the written word is put into the context of a larger literacy landscape.

Lesson Three

Questions, interpretations and dramatic devices

The third lesson consolidated and built on the work so far. I wanted to see if, now the children had heard one of the stories, they had anything to add to the description of Anancy they had explored in Salkey's poem. I also aimed to encourage them to question and interpret the story from different perspectives. Folk-tales contain many ambiguities, as Joe Winston identified (1998), and the relationship between comic playfulness and moral action gives pupils an opportunity to explore ethical issues. I wanted the children to engage in just such a debate, from their own point of view, and from that of a range of characters in the story, including Anancy himself.

In the first part of the lesson, we re-read Salkey's poem. The poem has, apparently, no defined narrative voice, and this was quickly established when I asked if they thought that any of the characters they had played in the previous lesson might have said these words. They recognised that it was an authorial voice in the poem, and this led them to ask about how James Berry and Andrew Salkey knew about Anancy. I had planned to look at the writers' sources for their work later, but as it had been raised it seemed appropriate to deviate from my lesson plan and read with them the first part of Berry's introduction to the *Anancy-Spiderman* stories. In this, he acknowledges 'Mother Africa', his ancestors, his parents, folklorist Louise Bennett, writer Walter Jekyll and his publisher. As the children listed the people who had influenced him, it became clear that the stories had travelled and changed; this insight provided a context for the work which followed. One girl described how she first heard about Anancy from her grandmother, but that although Anancy was the same in the stories she had heard, she told the class that in other stories, he was better at his tricks. Returning to my plan, the children looked back at the lists of adverbs and adjectives they had complied in the previous lesson, and compared them with the portrait of Anancy they had first read in Salkey's poem. The ensuing questions about what writers can change and what they can leave out, was central to their understanding of the genre, and we wrote a 'recipe' for the Anancy tales which gave a basis for the drama which followed.

Because I was interested in the moral issues implicit in the story, and the ways in which the various characters represent different viewpoints and moral positions, we returned to the story of *Mrs Anancy, Chicken Soup and Anancy*. I gave the class writing frames, which were based on Salkey's poem. Writing frames, as Webster, Beveridge and Reed (1996) point out, provide the scaffolding for children's literacy learning, and help them to develop a repertoire of written styles. In this particular context, the writing frame had a number of purposes; it would lead the children to consider different viewpoints, it would encourage economy of style; it would focus their attention on the development of plot in relation to character. The writing frames were differentiated according to ability, although all were based on part of Salkey's poem, with words missed out. Their job was to substitute words to describe Anancy, but also to decide who might be saying them and at what point in the story. This poem would then be used as a dramatic script. Having explained the whole task, I structured the work into more manageable units.

The children's first job was to decide where the scene would be, and who would be in it. From this they developed an improvisation, which they used in the writing. There were a variety of responses to this task – the children created a gleeful scene where Bro Dog puts on his disguise; a conversation between the children at the feast; and a rather surreal discussion between two chickens. To illustrate their work, I have chosen two examples. The writing frame has been indicated in bold.

Joe and Stacey, who have some literacy difficulties, worked on a monologue describing Anancy's journey through the forest to the doctor's surgery. They had worked previously on this part of the story, and had used some imaginative movement to suggest that Anancy scuttled through the wood as a spider.

Their writing also built on the movement piece they had developed in response to the poem.

Where does the scene take place?
In the wood.
What are the characters doing?
Anancy drops his top hat and turns into a spider. He is talking to himself to feel big.
What has happened before this scene takes place?
He has pretended to be ill.

Anancy: **Sometimes, he is** grand
Sometimes, he is mysterious
Sometimes, he turns into a spider and gets free again.

Anancy is free
Anancy is trapped
Sometimes he tricks people.

Stacey and Joe both performed this short monologue. Stacey began, saying the lines as Anancy as a man, they both spoke the line 'Sometimes, he turns into a spider and gets free again', and Joe took over for the final lines where Anancy became a spider. Their use of the contrasting words 'free and trapped' showed understanding of antonyms and, notably, their work demonstrated an understanding of character. They recognised, and physicalised, the two sides of Anancy's personality, and their direction, 'he is talking to himself to feel big' implied a dramatic motive and understanding of plot and situation.

Emma and Jessie, who are confident writers, explored the scene where Mrs Anancy invites Dora and 24 children to a chicken feast. They told me that they were particularly drawn to this moment in the story because, 'it's the sort of thing you'd like to do to get back at people'.

Where does the scene take place?
The scene takes place in Dora's kitchen.
What are the characters doing?
Dora is peeling potatoes. Mrs Anancy is hot and bothered as she has just finished killing chickens.
What has happened before this scene takes place?
Mrs Anancy has got cross with Anancy because he has lied to her about being ill.

Mrs Anancy: **Sometimes, he is** so ugly and full of lies.
Dora: **Sometimes, he is** very greedy, Mrs Anancy, and thinks he is grand.
Mrs Anancy: **Sometimes, he** thinks I am a fool!
              But I will teach him a lesson.

Mrs Anancy whispers to Dora.

Dora: **Anancy is** not so clever as he thinks!
Mrs Anancy: **Tremendously** greedy.
Dora: **Excessively** stupid.

Mrs Anancy: **Sometimes, he is** selfish when he is feeling hungry.
Dora: **Sometimes, he is** a very jealous man.
Mrs Anancy: **Sometimes, he** tricks other people but I can trick him back.

What does the audience know at the end of the scene that they didn't know at the beginning?
That Mrs Anancy plans to trick Anancy.

This script revealed the children's literacy learning in a variety of ways. They had understood the viewpoints of different characters in the story, and their use of evaluative language – 'greedy', 'stupid', 'selfish', 'jealous' – made this clear. They, too, used antonyms in Dora's dialogue by juxtaposing 'clever' and 'stupid'. They also showed considerable consistency of role, and the relationship between the characters was symbolised by Mrs Anancy's judicious repetition of Dora's word, 'greedy'. In terms of the playwright's craft, their work demonstrated a range of dramatic devices: how to use stage directions to withhold information to an audience (Mrs Anancy whispers her plan to Dora); the use of both a set-up and pay-off in the last line, where one issue is resolved (that Mrs Anancy will trick Anancy); and an agenda for the next scene is set up (how will she do it?), with appropriate dramatic tension.

In the writing of the scenes, moral judgements on Anancy's actions were given not by children themselves, but were spoken by other characters in the story. As a final exercise, I asked them to find phrase from each of their scenes which showed Anancy's faults. Putting the top hat, cane and waistcoat in a circle to symbolise Anancy, they repeated these phrases as if they were talking to him. Noting the angry tone of voice, and accompanying gestures, I asked them how they would feel about Anancy if they were watching this as a play. They said they would feel sorry for him. It was a moral decision which I wanted to explore in the next lesson.

Lesson Four

A Community of Storytellers

Before this lesson, the children had completed two tasks. In school time, they had looked up information about the slave trade in information books and on CD-ROM, and pictures were displayed on the wall. They had also each read another Anancy-Spiderman story by James Berry. The school had a scheme to encourage parents to read to children at home, and this was particularly helpful. Arriving at the lesson, the children were keen to share their stories, and grouped according to the story they had read, they prepared to re-tell the story to the class by making notes. To help them frame their ideas, I read part of James Berry's introduction, and suggested that the children might miss out bits or expand on others. As this would take some time, we agreed to hear a story each day, a practise which continued after the project had finished and which allowed them all to reflect on the differences between oral and written narratives. It was in the process of selecting material that they understood how the drama had enabled them to get to know Anancy. There was no need for lengthy explanations because, as one boy said, 'we've met him before now, and other stories help us to know him a bit better'. The class had become a community of storytellers.

To remind them of the moral dimension of the previous lesson, we repeated the word exercise where they addressed Anancy. Particularly now that they had heard another story, they felt sorry for Anancy, and wanted to hear his side of the story. The children took on the role of villagers, working in the fields and, in role as Anancy, I put on the costume. I gathered the children around me, and told the story of *Mrs Anancy, Chicken Soup and Anancy* entirely from Anancy's perspective. They asked me questions and, following the children's cues, a dramatised version of Anancy's motives became clear. Still in role, I asked them to return to their work in the fields, and to tell each other my story. As they mimed feeding chickens and cutting crops, each child took it in turns to tell part of Anancy's story.

Out of role, I asked the children if they thought that the stories would be improved if the explanation of Anancy's actions were included. They decided that, by and large, the stories did not need an explanation. The children noted that a resolution which depended on seeing the action from Anancy's point of view, though satisfying in dramatic terms, was not part of the oral tradition of storytelling, where audiences are left to make up their own minds. It was at this point that I knew that they had understood the social and cultural purpose of the oral tradition where, as James Tully (1995) argues, there is an implicit ambiguity in the moral message, which invites interpretation precisely because it leaves the audience with unanswered questions.

In concluding the project, I decided to consolidate the children's learning by drawing together the dramatic elements into an impromptu performance. This would enable the children to reflect on the work they had achieved, and it gave me the opportunity to explore further the historical and cultural context of the Anancy stories. In terms of sentence level work, this also gave the children an opportunity to work on the punctuation in their written scripts, which had lacked a sense of the play in performance. Using another writing frame, I asked them to finish the play by writing a five line script in which Anancy explained his actions to another character. This would include stage directions to indicate gestures and movement, and punctuation which suggested intonation, pauses and hesitancy. Jasmine and Peter's script is a good example.

Anancy:	It wasn't my fault, honestly.
Mrs Anancy:	Oh . . . what? You are saying you couldn't help it. LIAR!
Anancy:	Um . . . I . . . I . . . (*quietly*) I felt really hungry.
Mrs Anancy:	(*shouting*) ANANCY! TELL ME THE TRUTH! (*she calms down*) You wanted to steal my chickens.
Anancy:	Steal? Me!? The truth? The truth is I only wanted to have a nice dinner with you, my dear. A celebration. (*Mrs Anancy frowns and crosses her arms*)

This script, written under time constraints, demonstrates in context an understanding of punctuation and stage directions. The children also recognised that, written in this way, other actors might interpret their script in the way they intended. Adding specifically dramatic vocabulary to their spelling logs – gesture, intonation, facial expression – drew their attention to the different audiences for playscripts, that information for actors is included both within the dialogue and in extra-dialogic instructions.

The final 'presentation' included different elements of the work. The class performed Salkey's poem; they re-told *Mrs Anancy, Chicken Soup and Anancy* in movement with onomatopoeic 'found poems'; they improvised scenes, with scripted dialogue, to show different characters' points of view; they mimed villagers working in the fields, telling Anancy's story, and enacted duologues showing Anancy's explanation. At the end of the performance, I came into the drama in role, as a storyteller. Using the pictures they had gathered about the slave trade, I began to tell the storyteller's story, about how and why these stories were told. As the children listened, I referred to the pictures of the slaves they had found, many of them disturbing. Anancy had, during the four days, become a friend, and the story of his stories was one I felt they should know.

In the final reflections on the work, I asked them why they thought Anancy's stories had survived so long. Joe and Jessie understood. 'Because they told them to make themselves feel big, like Anancy, and now they are told to remember what it was like'. Our play had no title, I said. I asked them if they could find any suitable words in their spelling logs or on the wall. The title they chose was 'A Special Kind of Freedom'.

Bibliography

Berry, J., *Anancy-Spiderman*, Walker Books, 1986.

Bryant, P., *Children's Reading Problems*, Basil Blackwell, 1985.

Fielding, M., 'Why and How Learning Styles Matter' in Hart, S. (ed) *Differentiation and the Secondary Curriculum*, Routledge, 1996.

Kress, G., *Learning to Write*, Routledge, 1982.

Meek, M., *On Being Literate*, Bodley Head, 1991.

National Literacy Strategy, The DfEE, 1988.

Salkey, A., 'Anancy' poem in Grace Nichols *Black Poetry*, Blackie, 1988.

Tully, J., *Strange Multiplicities*, Cambridge University Press, 1995.

Webster, A., Beveridge, M. & Reed, M. *Managing the Literacy Curriculum*, Routledge, 1996.

Winston, J., *Drama, Narrative and Moral Education*, The Falmer Press. 1998.

Lesson Guide – Anancy-Spiderman

Resources Large rolls of paper, plain paper, felt pens, pencils, dictionaries, top hat, waistcoat, cane, worksheets of writing frames, complete copies of

Andrew Salkey's poem *Anancy*, and copies of third and forth stanza cut up for group work; copies of James Berry's book *Anancy-Spiderman*.

Time The lesson guide covers four separate literacy hours for Year 5 Term 2, with an additional research task of 30 minutes, and a reading task of 20 minutes.

Literacy Learning Word Level 1, 10, 11. Sentence Level 3, 6. Text Level 1, 2, 3, 5, 8, 11, 12, 14, 17, 18.

Lesson One

* **Reading props:** Lay out top hat, waistcoat and cane on the floor. Class speculate about their owner. One child to try them on. All walk in a manner suggested by the props, and describe how they feel.
* **Teacher reading:** Read Andrew Salkey's poem *Anancy* to the class. Remember to use props.
* **Movement:** Individually, children travel to four areas of the room, showing Anancy in top hat, carrying cane, wearing waistcoat and turning into a spider. In groups, prepare moving image and saying lines from stanzas 3 or 4. Read the last stanza, children make an image to match words. Put whole poem together as a performance.
* **Role on the wall:** Draw round a child on large paper and draw in top hat. Class record adjectives to describe Anancy as a man on his body, and adverbs to describe his movement on his arms and legs. In pairs, on the paper outside the image, write down antonyms to describe what he is like as a spider. Put on wall.
* **Reflection:** In a circle, class share ideas of Anancy's character and the contrast between spider and man.

Year 5 • Term 2
T5, 1
W10

111

Lesson Two

* **Teacher reading:** Read *Mrs Anancy, Chicken Soup and Anancy*. Ask class to join in groans and other onomatopoeic words/phrases.
* **Mapping the story:** In groups, children draw a map of a particular section of the story.
* **Still images:** In same groups, children create three still images each to show action in their scene.
* **Found poems:** Still in groups, find onomatopoeic words in the story which are added to still images. Record these words in spelling logs. Class perform the scenes to tell the whole story.

Year 5 • Term 2
T5
W11

* **Reflection:** Class asked to speculate on genre of the story. Find words to show how the mood and atmosphere changes as the story develops.

Lesson Three

Year 5 • Term 2
T8, 4, 5
S3

* **Teacher reading:** Re-read Salkey's poem *Anancy*. Put props on the floor as a visual reminder.
* **Class discussion:** Class discuss if any of the characters in the story might have written the poem. Discuss possibilities, and why.
* **Teacher reading:** Read the first part of James Berry's introduction to *Anancy-Spiderman*. Scribes list all the people he thanks on sugar paper. Class invited to speculate about history of these stories, and how they might have changed over time.
* **Writing recipe:** Class add to the description of Anancy on role on the wall, then write a collective recipe which includes all the ingredients of an Anancy story, based on their knowledge so far.
* **Writing frames:** Explain whole task – children will write a scene in pairs, using part of the poem with words missed out. First decide: who is talking to Anancy? What does he or she think of Anancy? When in the story does this scene take place? Put these questions on board. In pairs, children improvise scenes, then fill in writing frame. Each pair performs the scene.
* **Talking to Anancy:** Put props which symbolise Anancy in a circle, children choose one line from their scenes to say to him, with suitable intonation and gesture. Class copies each line and gesture after each leader.
* **Reflection:** Class discuss what they now know about Anancy as a character, and how an audience might feel about him, following the last exercise. Record vocabulary in spelling log.

Lesson Four

Year 5 • Term 2
T3, 12, 8, 5, 2, 18
S6

* **Teacher reading:** Read last three paragraphs of James Berry's introduction to *Anancy-Spiderman*. Explain that they too can miss bits out when they re-tell an Anancy story, or add to it if they like.
* **Pupil storytelling:** In groups, pupils prepare to retell one of the stories from Berry's book, *Anancy-Spiderman* by making notes. One group tell the story.
* **Teacher in role:** Class in role as villagers in the fields. Teacher in role as Anancy tells the story from his point of view. Remember to embellish by including parts of the story children have just told.
* **Spotlighting:** Class in role as villagers, retelling Anancy's version of the story in groups. Spotlight groups to hear snapshots of conversation.

* **Script writing:** In pairs, children use writing frame to write script in which Anancy explains his actions to another character. Scripts should show intonation, pauses and gesture through stage directions and punctuation. On wall, write up dramatic vocabulary such as rehearsal, gesture, facial expression, intonation for their spelling logs. Children show scenes to another pair.

* **Performance:** Class put together poem, story telling with onomatopoeic poems, scenes about Anancy, mime with snapshots of Anancy's version, and scenes of Anancy's explanation. Make sure all children show some of their group or pair work.

* **Teacher as Storyteller:** Children gather round pictures of slave trade. Referring to the pictures, tell them the story of how the Anancy stories were told in their original context, as a form of resistance. Ask them to give their play a title.

* **Reflection (additional time):** Children consolidate their learning by sharing ideas about Anancy, reflecting on which parts of the drama worked best and why, about how they have changed the story, and by recording all the new vocabulary they have learnt in the project. Refer to assessment criteria, and ask the children to evaluate their own learning.

113

The Gargoyles Creep
•using•
Night of the Gargoyles by Eva Bunting

Joe Winston is a lecturer in the Department of Arts Education at the University of Warwick. His publications include Beginning Drama and Drama, Narrative and Moral Education.

This work was developed for children in the upper primary age range. It has also been trailed by groups of teachers and trainee teachers who have used it as part of their own teaching. It was originally devised for a teacher in a school that timetabled one week's break per term from the normal pattern of the literacy hour. As such it was experimental, investigating how the arts might contribute to children's literacy. The school intends to build similar weekly projects into each year group once a term.

Written examples later in the chapter feature the work of children from Year 5 of Dorridge Junior School. I am grateful to them and to their teachers, Marie Cameron, Glenn Duggan and Norma Lewis.

The Project

Night of the Gargoyles is written by Eve Bunting and illustrated in black and white by David Wiesner. The opening lines provide us with a flavour of the poetic qualities of its language and the eerie atmosphere it generates:

> The gargoyles squat
> high on corners
> staring into space,
> their empty eyes unblinking
> till night comes.

Its narrative relates how, every night, the gargoyles awaken and explore their environment. They jump across rooftops, peer into the windows of the museum whose roof they adorn, fly or crawl down into the empty streets below where, around the fountain in the centre of a deserted square, they meet with other gargoyles from different rooftops. Here they complain of the life humans have made for them. Immobile during the day, they are condemned to squat on high, exposed to all weathers, unable to brush off the birds that irritate them, having to endure the hot sun and the choking rain. They have no love of humans, we are told, and we see them pursue and frighten a security guard, whose employer doesn't believe that he has seen the gargoyles move. Their pursuit is not malicious, however; they simply pull faces and squawk at him and the narrative concludes with the gargoyles returning quietly to their rooftops once more, where they are condemned to stare and stare ... till night comes once again.

The illustrations are as important as the text in evoking the eerie but comic atmosphere of the tale. Their black and white tones evoke the darkness and shadow of the old, moonlit city with its gothic skyline. The grotesque features of the gargoyles are at once fearsomely ugly and childishly naïve. Their expressions of complaint, discomfort and puzzlement are endearingly comic, and children are led to sympathise with these clumsy creatures of stone and can understand their scorn for humans who have made them as they are. Herein lies the moral thrust of the poem – a symbolic glimpse at the life of a community of outsiders, upon whom humans have projected their own fantasies of evil and horror. The gargoyles are creatures of the dark in more than one sense.

If the pictures are what can captivate and draw children into this world of the gargoyles, the powerful text contains many subtle qualities that reward exploration. Rhymes are sparse and the poetry works through alliteration, assonance and subtly shifting rhythms:

> They gargoyle-hunch around the rim
> and gargoyle-grunt
> with friends from other corners
> who have come for company.

I initially taught these sessions for roughly an hour a day over the period of a week. The classroom was quite spacious and the children were used to working with the desks pushed back. For some of the sessions, however, we were able to use the hall when we needed greater freedom of movement. The 'narrative' of these sessions is presented below and attempts to create an overall impression of the project rather than a detailed account of how the work was taught and organised. These details are presented in the much more thorough lesson guides at the end of the chapter.

The children were very excited when, for the first session, the classroom was in near total darkness and I presented the book in slide form, projected onto the wall. The atmosphere was enhanced by the eerie and repetitive strains of Christopher Benstead's *Nightwalking*, which played as I read the text. After gathering the children's enthusiastic initial responses to the poem I explained that our work for this week would be to explore and create the gargoyle world together through our bodies and through our words. I then explained that I was going to read a small section of the poem to show how we can play with the music of words in order to do this. I chose the section near the beginning where the gargoyles awaken and begin to move over the rooftops and read the first few lines as follows:

Then there's movement	(with a 2 second pause after 'Then')
In the shadowy corners	(whispering 'shadowy corners')
As the gargoyles creep	(lengthening the 'ee' in 'creep' and adding the rhythm of soft footfalls – 'cree – ee – ee- eep')
On stubs of feet	(staccato, for 'stubs of feet' – 'stubs – of – feet' followed by a sharp intake of breath)
Along the high ledges	(noticeably raising the pitch of my voice for 'high ledges')

Children then copied my reading line by line as I conducted them and, after discussing what I had done to the words and why, we wrote it out in a way that might illustrate how it should be read – small print for a whisper, a space representing a pause etc. Children then prepared and shared their own sections that were read with the lights dimmed and the blinds drawn.

I began our second session by reading though the text again, this time asking children to look out for the verbs that describe the noises the gargoyles make. After listing these on the board, I chose one of them – *grunt* – and together we explored ways in which we could make the sound of the grunt in the way we spoke it; or in the way we could select and speak parts of it – *grrr; unnn; rnnn;* and so on. In small groups, children experimented with the different gargoyle ways this and other words could be expressed. The class was then divided in half and each half in turn had to create the feel of the gargoyle world for the other through sound alone. As one half of the class sat in the centre of the space with its eyes closed, the other half created a sound collage that rose and fell, grew to climax and died away. I assisted by conducting the class, indicating when they might perform their sounds softly, when there might be moments of complete silence. This was reciprocated by the other half of the class and children discussed which effects they found most effective. The general agreement was that the moments of silence were particularly suspenseful and the noisiest moments would not have been as frightening without the quieter, whispering effects.

The next two lessons concentrated on movement rather than sound and took place in the hall. In the first we had a lot of fun pulling gargoyle faces, making up our own and copying those made by others. These activities had to be carefully structured to maintain control but this increased the amount fun children were able to have. They then incorporated these faces into a physicalisation of gargoyle shapes, which they worked on in 'huddles' of four. Torches and a darkened room helped create an eerie atmosphere when children shared their work, and this balance of the comic and the sinister in this lesson was meant to reflect the same balance so evident within the book itself. The following lesson moved from body shape to movement. Once again, I took the vocabulary of the poem as our starting point, this time using the variety of words in the poem that describe how the gargoyles move. The session was structured to encourage children to find abstract forms of movement, relating more to the musicality of the words than to any simplistic, mimetic portrayal of gargoyles in motion. The intention was to avoid the hackneyed and the obvious, to find surprising and new ways of playing with the kinds of movement possibilities suggested by the text.

For the final two lessons we moved back to the story. First of all, why did the gargoyles have no love of humans? This was an important area to explore as it lies at the heart of the moral theme of the text. I listed the children's suggestions then, with their help, I wrote them as a series of complaints that they could then shout at me angrily, as the only human in the room!

What revenge, therefore, might the gargoyles take on their creators? This question allowed us to explore the mischievous side of the gargoyles' nature and proved to be very appealing to the children, especially the boys. What kind of tricks might gargoyles play on humans to frighten rather than harm them? Where? This activity was framed as our chance to create extra pages for the text, written in the same poetic style as the author's. In groups, children had to first of all decide on a suitable trick and then show, through creating still images, how the artist could illustrate it in two, clear pictures. One group of children, for example, chose for their first image to show a restaurant with a waiter about to serve two gargoyles sat at table, their faces hidden in newspapers. In the second image, the gargoyles had jumped on to the tables and were grimacing at the waiter and at the other guests who were all in various states of shock – one having fainted, one leaning back in horror, one fleeing from the scene.

Having created the images, children moved on to work either in groups or as individuals on a piece of text to accompany them. The requirements for individual children were differentiated and some children produced two or three drafts before the final version. This was a concentrated piece of writing and was intended to help children understand that, in poetry, fewer words are often better than more words. The class teacher displayed these additional pages of the book, illustrated and with photographs, around her classroom.

Later, as part of an end of term school production, her class performed a version of *The Night of the Gargoyles*. As so much of the work covered over this week had had a performance element built into it, she found this very straightforward to bring about. And Year 5 were highly delighted to have this opportunity to attempt to frighten teachers, parents and children alike!

Learning Objectives

The activities are suitable for children in Year 5 and/or 6 and examine the verbal and visual qualities of a lengthy, illustrated poem that is very strong on atmosphere. They are intended to help children enjoy the poetry by exploring and playing with the atmosphere evoked through the texture and music of the language. The overall aim was to help bring alive the imaginary world of the poem through close attention to the words and pictures of the text and to enable children to write in the style of the author. All the activities reinforce reading, oracy and writing skills in a variety of ways. The lesson guides show how these aims are translated into specific objectives. In effect, the lessons were planned with a series of twin objectives in both drama and literacy, the one being intended to reinforce the other.

Assessment

Records of the children's oral and visual work were gathered at specific points in ways that were simple and manageable: still image work was photographed; group sound collages were tape recorded; the final performance work was videoed. This provided the teacher with evidence to inform assessment of the performative and presentational objectives detailed in the National Literacy Strategy descriptors. Written work was built into the programme and was assessed against those descriptors relating to children's appreciation of and ability to write poetry.

Sequence of Activities

Activity 1: Reading the story

This is best done through overhead transparencies or, if possible, slides. Although this necessitates some additional teacher preparation, the increased size of the images will make their impact on children that much more telling. Overhead transparencies (OHTs) can be used in a number of ways for text-based work. For example, we played *Kim's Game*, covering up words or phrases while the children closed their eyes, then asked me to tell them what is missing. Slides, on the other hand, can be projected as a backdrop to accompany some of the children's movement work. You will need good blackout facilities for slides to work effectively, however, but in a darkened room, they make for a particularly memorable first reading, especially when accompanied by atmospheric music. You are best advised to practise this reading in advance, experimenting with volume, tone and pace to create an edge of eerie expectation in your voice.

Activity 2: Exploring the musicality of the text

I prepared a section of the text – about eight lines – for a 'scored' reading. In such a reading you play with the verbal dynamics by emphasising and exaggerating the musicality of the words. You can whisper or shout some words or phrases, lengthen or clip the vowel sounds, raise or lower the pitch of your voice, add pauses or other sound effects – a rumbling laugh, a squawk, an intake of breath and so on.

I explained to the children before the reading that I would deliberately play with the music of the words. I read it through a second time, this time line by line, asking the children to repeat each line exactly as I read it. I also used gesture for emphasis; for example, two fingers of one hand creep through the air to accompany the rhythm of the word 'creep'; raising my hand to my mouth, as if in fright; looking over the children's heads and pointing upwards for a phrase such as 'high ledges'.

Having done this, I pointed to single lines at random and asked for individual volunteers to read them in the same manner. I encouraged the class to articulate what I had been doing with my voice and why – how the voice can be used to add colour and atmosphere to the reading. We then explored together how we could write the verse in such a way that graphically reflected how it was to read.

The children worked together in groups to prepare a reading of a small section of the text, copying my techniques and adding some of their own. When this was done, each child wrote a graphic version to show how it should be read. After one final rehearsal, we shared the readings with the class.

Activity 3: Word collage

I went through the complete text of *The Night of the Gargoyles*, page by page with the whole class, asking children to point out words that describe the sounds the gargoyles make. These should include: 'grunt', 'grump', 'lap', 'split-splat', 'rumble laugh', 'rasp', 'stomp' and 'scream'. We then listed these words on the board and I divided the class into as many groups as there were words (i.e. there are eight words listed here; in a class of 32 children, that gave us eight groups of four). Each group was given a word and they explored different 'gargoyle' ways of expressing it, using the word or parts of the word. After a few minutes these were shared.

I now divided the class into two by dividing each group in half. This ensured that there were samples of each sound in each half of the class. Sitting half of the class in the centre of the room, the other half were placed in a circle around them. The challenge for the children in the circle was to create the gargoyle world for those in the centre through sound alone. This worked best with a darkened room, with children in the centre closing their eyes for the duration of the activity. With children inexperienced in this kind of work you should conduct it, raising your hand to raise the volume, bringing different children in and out of the collage at different times. In order to manage this successfully you will need to have a series of agreed signals that children can understand and follow. If the class is used to such work, you can ask children to decide for themselves when to come in and out of the collage and at what volume. You can also introduce movement, with children having the choice of travelling in the space around the group in the centre.

Once the collage is performed, discuss with the children in the centre the images, the sounds conjured up and the feelings the activity induced in them. Then each half of the class can swap over and the exercise can be repeated.

Activity 4: Gargoyle faces

To open the session, we looked at a selection of pictures of gargoyles on the OHT. I pointed to some of the particularly expressive faces, and asked the children to mirror them as a whole class. Returning to the faces on the OHT, we discussed what the gargoyles might be thinking, saying or feeling.

In a circle, we played *Pass the Mask*. Start with one child who pulls a gargoyle face and passes it to the person on their left. This person must mirror that mask, then turn their face into the centre of the circle, drop this mask and replace it with a new one of their own. The game continues in this way around the circle and can be accompanied by some suitably ironic music, such as 'All Things Bright and Beautiful'. Although humorous, this musical commentary makes a serious dramatic point by evoking ironically the ugliness that human beings have deliberately cast upon the gargoyles.

In groups of four, I then asked the children to create gargoyle huddles. In each huddle, the children faced in the same direction and were at different levels. I asked them to attempt to convey menace through their body postures as well as through their faces. These group sculptures can be studied and commented on. This worked particularly well by giving a torch or two to each group and, making the room as dark as possible, asking each group to use the torches to light up their faces. The distorted effects of light and shadow on grotesque face-pulling was very effective.

Activity 5: Gargoyles in motion

The following list of verbs which describe how the gargoyles move was taken from the poem, and shown to the children: 'creep', 'fly', 'swing', 'swoop', 'crawl'. In the text these verbs are often prefixed with the word 'gargoyle' – 'they gargoyle-creep', for example. The children read the list of words, repeating this prefix each time. I then asked them to add other verbs of motion to the list. These initially included simple words like 'run' and 'walk', but I encouraged children to find more expressive words such as 'leap', 'slither', 'scramble' and 'hobble'. When we were happy with the list, we discussed the meaning of the word 'contrast', and I asked them to volunteer pairs of words where the movements contrast with one another – 'fly' and 'crawl,' for example, or 'leap' and 'creep'. The children chose two such contrasting words, and then I asked them to repeat them silently in their heads with the prefix 'gargoyle' added to each: 'I gargoyle fly and gargoyle crawl', for example, or 'I gargoyle leap and gargoyle creep'. Then I asked the class to say these words all at once and, once sure each child had their own phrases to work with, introduced the idea of 'taking the phrase for a walk'. Here children move freely in space, playing with the musicality of the phrases in a variety of ways, using the kind of strategies described in Lesson One above. Once they found a way of uttering the phrase that they were happy with, they sat down in a space and waited for everyone else to finish. When this happened, I asked the class to repeat their phrases to me all at once.

To develop this further, I requested that the children resume the exercise only this time adding movement to the phrase. It is important that they appreciate this is *not* a mimed exercise. Every word is to be accompanied by movement of an abstract sort, suggested by the *musicality* of the words. Once children understand this, they should have little problem with it. You can help children by specifying, for example that their movement phrases (or *motifs*) must involve travel across the floor; a turn; and a change of level. As with the previous exercise, the children played with ideas before refining them into a rehearsed motif that they could perform time and time again, without stopping or interrupting the flow of their movement. Once they were confident that they had done this, they could drop the verbal phrases they began with, so that we were left only with the movement. Half the class now showed their work to the other half, those watching being invited to comment on particular aspects of what they saw that they liked.

There are a number of ways that can be chosen to develop this work. You can, for example, ask every child to find a partner to whom they will show their motif and then ask each pair to choose one of the two that they will learn to perform together. You can say that you would like it performed twice, once in unison and once in canon (where one child starts the motif slightly later than the other). This simple sequence, together with each child's individual motif, can be used to improvise a semi-structured dance as follows:

1 Children begin as individuals, still, in space. When the music begins, they use their individual motifs to travel across the floor.
2 On meeting with their partners they must first of all pause to make eye contact, perform their joint piece together, then move away again. This sequence can be improvised two or three times and each time the relationship in space can be different – performing close to one's partner can be followed by performing from some distance. The dance can be accompanied by the same atmospheric music used for the initial reading of the poem and children should be asked to listen closely to it as they perform, allowing it to influence the quality of their movement.

They have no love of humans who have made them so . . .

They huddle mischievously,
And plan sweet revenge . . .
Ha Ha Ha!
Then gargoyle steal and slither,
Silently into town,
Where stony fingers slink,
Slowly to their target.

Then froth, fizz, and sshh,
Startled humans can't believe their eyes.
As frothy beer and bubbles rise,
And deep grumbly gargoyle sniggers
echo in the fading night.

David Clinton Joshua Devey James Billington Gabriel Taghi

Activity 7, see page 125

They have no love of humans who have made them so . . .

They creep to the theatre to see
the evening show.
Shoelaces tied and . . .
. . . round two steal
and spy some feet.
Poise ready to pounce while
up several fly to view.

Then gargoyle secrete themselves
away from human sight
as the trick goes into action.
The show is now over
a human rises from his seat.

ROLL! CRASH! TUMBLE!
pandemonium breaks out
they hoot with gargoyle laughter
as some swoop down and scare humans
witless.
People scream as a tingling icy fear overcomes
them
chaos still reigns as the gargoyle sneaks away

Raveen Dhillon Edward Moss Jenny Hall Louise Cave James Purchase Tim Hill Adrian Chan

Activity 7, see page 125

Activity 6: 'They have no love of humans' (1)

Referring the children to the section of the text that tells how the gargoyles have no love of humans, we brainstormed all the reasons why this is the case. The poem, for example, tells us that they don't like being exposed to the sun, being choked by autumn leaves, or having to endure the loud sounds of the clock. Under the heading 'Why gargoyles have no love of humans' we noted these reasons. To stretch the children, I asked for some reasons that are implied rather than spelt out – because humans made them ugly, for example; humans made them unable to move, humans made them outcasts, etc. Then I asked them to consider how we often accuse people by asking questions beginning with the word 'Why?' 'Why are you making so much noise?', 'Why did you borrow my pen without asking?'. Using the notes made so far, I asked for suggestions of what questions of this nature the gargoyles might pose to humans – 'Why do you make me sit in the sun all day?', 'Why did you make me so ugly?', 'Why are we unwanted and alone?', 'What have we done to deserve this?' are all examples of the kind of complaints the children constructed in this exercise.

When we had a good list of complaints, we read through it as a whole class, experimenting with different ways of emphasising the complaints – by shouting, whining prodding the air with our finger. The children then chose in silence one of these complaints and memorised it. On a given signal, I asked the whole class to complain to me altogether. Once again, they were encouraged to adopt physical postures and facial expressions to accompany the way they chose to voice their complaints.

Activity 7: 'They have no love of humans' (2)

I suggested to the children that the authors might like to add a further two pages towards the end of the book. This double page would have two illustrations and a section of text to show how the gargoyles carry out some mischievous acts of revenge on humans by going to places where humans like to gather at night in order to play tricks on them. We discussed and drew up a list of what these places might be. The list included service stations, pubs, restaurants, cinemas, night clubs, all-night car parks, and late night supermarkets. We then brainstormed ideas of what kind of tricks the gargoyles might play on the humans.

I now divided the class into groups of five, and the children worked out still images to represent the two illustrations. The first showed the gargoyles setting up the trick, the second showed its results. The children then showed these images to the rest of the class, moving from the first to the second at a given signal.

Having performed the 'trickery', I asked the children to create the text to accompany these images. They were by now well acquainted with the tone and language of the poem, but this proved a good point to look at or revise certain of its characteristics – the shortness of the lines; the use of the prefix 'gargoyle' to describe the creatures' movements; the use of assonance and internal rhymes. At this stage, we split into different ability groups. Some children were required to produce just four lines of text, others eight lines; some asked to write a generalised passage of the gargoyles' antics, of which their illustration is just one example, others asked simply to describe what happened in their own images. I wanted to encourage the children to write in poetic form, rather than a simple narrative story. To encourage this, I selected one group's work, made an OHT of it and we worked together for 15 minutes on ways in which we could reduce the amount of words and use more expressive vocabulary. Then I encouraged the children to do the same with their own texts for homework. See pages 123 and 124 for some examples of children's writing taken from one class of Year 5.

Optional Performance

Building a performance

There is no need to feel compelled to share this work with the rest of the school but the building blocks are all here for a simple performance piece and they can be readily assembled as follows in about three sessions in the hall.

1 You will need a large area of floor space. If you are performing for a small audience, such as parents and governors, or to another class, you might consider sitting them in the middle of the hall and performing around them. If the audience is larger, it will be best to spread them thinly rather than deeply. Blackout facilities would be very effective but are not necessary. If they are available, or if you have the use of a back projector, you can project the slides on to a wall or a backdrop, changing them at various times throughout the performance.

2 Begin the performance with your reading of the story, as in Activity 1.

3 The children gather in various positions in the space and freeze. Half of the class are in 'gargoyle huddles' (as in Activity 4), the other half stand or

squat in various, individual gargoyle postures. There should be a variety of gesture and level.

4 The children, beginning with those in the huddles, build up a word/sound collage. When the single gargoyles join in they can travel through the space. The collage should build gradually and it should conclude with the single gargoyles moving out of the performance area, leaving only the huddled groups.

5 After a moment's silence start the tape of 'All Things Bright and Beautiful' to which the groups light up their 'gargoyle faces' with the torches. Some groups might move very close to the audience and make gargoyle faces at them.

6 Fade out the song and fade in 'Nightwalking'. At this, the groups can break up in a structured sequence to perform a version of the movement piece devised in Activity 5.

7 The music fades and the groups vacate the space to be replaced by the other half of the class who assemble to perform a selection of the images composed in Activity 7. These should be accompanied by recitations of the matching texts written by the children. These are best recited by children outside the image and can be spoken using the strategies explored in Activity 2.

8 When these are completed, fade in 'Nightwalking' once again to permit this half of the class to perform their movement sequences devised in Activity 5.

9 As the music fades for the final time, the children freeze in gargoyle shapes, then turn and look at the audience. In sequence, they ask the questions prepared in Activity 6, directly addressing the audience. The rest of the class enters and they, too, ask their gargoyle questions. When every child has done this there is a momentary pause before the whole class begins to ask them at once, slowly approaching the audience as they do so, their voices sounding more and more menacing. Suddenly the teacher turns off the lighting and there is silence and stillness. The performance ends.

Lesson Guide

Resources The book *Night of the Gargoyles*, by Eve Bunting and illustrated by David Wiesner, 'Nightwalking' by Christopher Benstead from *Music for Dance, Vol. 1*, 'All Things Bright and Beautiful' from *Hello Children, Everywhere, Vol. 1*.

Time Five hours teaching time with final performance project as an optional extra. Presented as a series of activities rather than as lessons.

Thus you may select from them at will and incorporate them into your planning as best fits your individual circumstances, timetabling restrictions and priorities.

Literacy Learning The work was done initially as a Year 5 project but some teachers have adapted it for Year 6, so I present sets of National Literacy Strategy objectives for both year groups below.

Year 5 Term 3
* to read, rehearse and modify performance poetry
* to write in the style of the author
* to use performance poems as models to write and produce poetry in polished forms through revising, redrafting and presentation

Year 6 Term 2
* to recognise how poets manipulate words:
    – 	for their quality of sound e.g. rhythm, rhyme, assonance
    – 	for their connotations
    – 	for multiple layers of meaning e.g. through figurative language, ambiguity.
* to analyse how messages, moods, feelings and attitudes are conveyed in poetry
* to analyse the success of texts and writers in evoking particular responses in the reader e.g. where suspense is well-built

In the case of the programme for Year 6, the activities *as a whole* support these descriptors in a cumulative fashion, rather than being directed discretely at each in turn. I have not tried to present an exhaustive range of reading and writing activities, but have concentrated on those that emphasise drama work. These can, of course, be supported by other approaches to textual study promoted by the National Literacy Strategy.

Activities

* **Activity 1 – Reading the story:** Use OHT or slides, covering up words/phrases – prediction.
* **Activity 2 – Musicality of text:** Prepare 8 lines for 'scored' reading. Exaggerate key words. Discussion of musicality of words; written assignment to show how it should be read. Volunteers read single lines. Groups prepare a reading.

- **Activity 3 – Word collage:** Read text page by page; children point out adjectives describing 'gargoyle sounds'. Make list of words, divide into groups to express words. Then two groups, one in centre, one in circle around centre. Those in circle have to create a 'gargoyle world' for those in centre through sound alone. Swap.

- **Activity 4 – Gargoyle faces:** Pictures of gargoyles on OHT. *Pass the mask* – with musical accompaniment. Create gargoyle huddles. Use torches for effect.

- **Activity 5 – Gargoyles in motion:** Show list of verbs describing 'gargoyle movement'. Children repeat words with 'gargoyle' prefix – encourage them to find more expressive words. Create 'contrast' list, and 'take phrase for a walk'. Now add movement, then drop verbal phrase and concentrate purely on movement.

- **Activity 6 – 'They have no love of humans (1)':** Brainstorm why gargoyles dislike humans and note down. Search for implied reasons. Experiment with ways of emphasising complaints. On signal, whole class to complain using voice, posture, facial expression.

- **Activity 7 – 'They have no love of humans (2)':** In groups of five, children to act out gargoyles' mischievous revenge on humans (still imaging). Create text to accompany images, as though for double-page spread in book. Encourage poetry rather than prose.

Planning Literacy Dramas

This book provides three possibilities for using drama for literacy learning. Firstly, there is the possibility of teaching the lessons in their entirety, as they are written in the Lesson Guides. They have been taught in this way by the authors and their teaching colleagues. Secondly, there is the option of using the texts with selected activities, not necessarily all of them, not in the order in which they appear in the Lesson Guides. There is also a third possibility: to use the same approaches with other texts. This chapter looks at three particular approaches and illustrates how you can devise your own dramas.

Teacher in Role

Here the teacher takes a part in the play with the children. In other words the teacher plays the role of a character in the dramatic fiction. The previous chapters have provided various examples of teacher roles in action. Sometimes teachers use objects or bits of costume to indicate when they are in role. They put them down when they are addressing the children as the teacher in the real world. This can make it exciting for children as well as avoiding confusion between the teacher and the pretend character. Boulton, for example, refers to using fabrics to signify different characters.

Tip 1

When preparing for a role, it is essential to be clear about the functions of the teacher role. There are always at least dual functions at play: one concerned with the children's learning of literacy, and the other one related to the drama. Take the example of the children meeting teacher in role as Giant at the beach in Boshell's drama. Here the pedagogic function is to practice persuasive language while the fictional function is to enable children to apologise and get Giant back.

Consider the teacher role of the little girl in the spelling activity described in Chapter 1. In terms of literacy, the teacher in role has multiple functions: to invite rhyming words; to motivate children to spell them; to identify incorrect spellings; to necessitate spelling correction. The fictional function is, of course, to further the story so the children can help the girl get back into the castle.

The teacher role may be to give information, to elicit information, to enable practice of a register or type of communication, to encourage consideration of a different point of view, or perhaps to invite the children into the story they are about to read. Miller remains in role for very long spells to support writing activities. On other occasions the function will require a much shorter encounter with a teacher role.

Tip 2

Given the function of your role, ensure that you know exactly what is expected of the children. In preparing the children to meet your role, be sure that they know what is expected of them. Are they to find out about something or someone? The children are invited to think of questions they could ask Rainbow Fish before they see him, in Boulton's drama. Are there things they need to be careful about when speaking to the role? Take Flemming's role of the Ostler. He cannot be accused of anything outright and indeed, might decide not to speak to them at all if the children get nasty with him.

Tip 3

Always be sure that there is a reason for the children to speak to your role, and that there is enough for them to work on. It may be that you introduce it to invite them into the drama out of curiosity. When Nicholson took the role of Anancy, the children have a clear reason for talking to him. They want to hear his version of events because they feel sorry for him. A common fear for teachers is that the dialogue between children and teacher in role will run dry. I often rehearse the possible conversations in my mind to be sure that there is enough for the children to 'go at'. The teacher can create obstacles so the children have to work harder. Perhaps the role is not prepared to tell them her secret straightaway. Perhaps she needs to know if they can be trusted first. When preparing the children for the role it needs to be clear that there is something that they do not know. This acts as a carrot to motivate them to speak to the character. If they already have all the information about the character, there is no reason to talk.

Tip 4

Do not be afraid of silence. The character may be shy to speak, or the subject matter may be difficult to explain. Leaving the children to find the right words to use may take a little time. Ask them direct questions to help them – 'Have you heard anybody saying anything about my father?' 'How do I know you are my friend?'

Creating a teacher role: example

Let us suppose you are doing *Jack and the Beanstalk* and you decide to take the role of Jack.

What function will the role perform? The fictional functions may include providing information about the giant who is lying at the foot of the beanstalk still alive and developing imaginative possibilities to further the story. Pedagogic functions may include encouraging children to find words to create a sympathetic discourse, engaging in prediction, and to generate descriptive writing. Jack will need to use a range of adjectives when he speaks about the giant. These may need to be repeated and added to so that the children's vocabularies will be extended. Writing a descriptive paragraph about the giant from what they discovered from Jack will help reinforce the children's acquisition of new adjectives.

How will the children know what they must do? You may tell them that Jack is hiding behind the old oak tree. You are sure he is crying and shaking with fear. You can't understand it. He will not speak to you. Perhaps he would speak to the children as they are nearer his own age. Would they try to calm him and find out what the problem is? Their task is clear: calm Jack and discover the problem. The problem for Jack to gradually explain is the presence of the giant!

What is the reason for them to speak to the role and is there enough to talk about? They will want to speak to Jack because he is sad. They will want to help him. The curiosity has been set up: why is he crying? A challenge has been set up for the children. The teacher has failed to get him to explain. Can the children succeed? Prepare in your mind possibilities to extend the conversation. Jack could be afraid that the others will be angry because he has put them at risk by bringing the giant to their village. He may feel guilty and wonder what he could give the giant to eat and drink. He could be worrying about how he could possibly get the giant back to his home in the sky since he has chopped down the bean stalk. He may need advice about what to do.

When may there be silences, and what might be difficult for the children? Jack may not be prepared to speak quickly. The children may need to think up alternative approaches to get Jack's confidence. They may need time to think about what to suggest.

Here, then a teacher in role has engaged children in a narrative which they create with the teacher. It has extended descriptive vocabulary and provided a motive for the children to use it. They can then create WANTED posters with detailed descriptions of the giant when they discover he has gone from where he fell.

Still Images

Children arrange themselves to form an image like a sculpture. Once in position the children do not move or speak. It is as though they are frozen. A still image may depict an idea, a photo, a dream, a hope or fear, a moment of the past, a picture, or much more. We have seen children creating still images to recreate pictures from story books, of pictures that might have been in the story books, and of imagined moments. You can use still images from almost anything: sounds, songs, stories, words, poems. Winston's class, for example, prepared images to depict the tricks that the gargoyles could get up to.

Tip 1

Again, be sure of the function. Boshell uses a still image of the initial picture of the beautiful Giant to set the scene where the story begins, and as a simple introduction to dramatic activity. The image also served as a way of pooling evocative language to describe the scene.

Tip 2

Decide how the still image will be carried out. The still image could be in pairs, in small groups, or with the whole class. It might be that you wish to create a range of images to depict different moments, as Miller did to create events in the life of Lila. To do this requires small group still images. However, to create a place or atmosphere in which the story will take place will be easier with a whole class still image.

Tip 3

Decide a method for creating the images. There are again, many possibilities. Small groups can be given a time limit or the count to ten. For a whole class image you may give five claps to indicate time for children to find a position and hold it. To set a scene where something is to take place, this is easy and quick. Alternatively, you may want to ensure that each child knows exactly where everyone else is and what they are doing. The class may begin in a circle and slowly one by one as indicated by the teacher, they move into the space and take a position.

Tip 4

When the still images have been created in pairs or small groups consider how best they can be presented. Miller brings them all together into one performance piece through using the teacher role looking at a photograph album. The groups create the still images as though they are the photographs that are being considered. They could be presented in a line to represent time passing, or spread around the space approached by the teacher in role in random order to signify different fears or hopes.

Creating still images – example

Let us suppose you are working from a poem about bullying.

What will be the functions? The image has multiple functions. The pedagogic function involves introducing alternative viewpoints to prepare for writing tasks. The dramatic function entails defining the space of our pretend playground in our real classroom.

How will the image be carried out? The subject of the poem is serious and sensitive. Letting children go off to work in groups relinquishes some of the teacher's potential to determine the attitude with which children approach the task. Engaging the whole class in one still image can help children to better focus and concentrate.

How will the image be created? It is the observers of bullying who are to be the focus of this image. But first, two children should be directed by the others into positions to depict one bullying the other. The others can stand around the edge of the space. You could narrate in order to set the scene.

> It was towards the end of break. It would have been hard to miss it. There was the scuffle, the shouting, the sudden movements. Some crowded round to jeer, others got as far away as they could whilst others pretended they didn't know; couldn't see. Each of you play a role of one who was there. Where were you at this moment? What were you doing?

It would be best to ask for silence as the whole class still image is created. One at a time the children around the edge can step into the space and take a position. The others will watch to see how each is positioned. Are they watching, moving away, going to tell a teacher? Some may place themselves in relation to those already in the image, making groups, whispering, pointing out to someone. The image will be complete when each child is in a position in the imaginary playground.

How will the still images be presented? In this whole group image, its slow deliberate creation is its presentation. The poem speaks of a character bullying and a character bullied. The still image has opened up an awareness of the perspective of everyone else present. There are now many more viewpoints from which to explore the events of the poem. The way the image requires a considered decision about where to go in the playground acts as a reminder that observers do make choices, just as bullies do. This may suggest some sense of responsibility for the observer. The emotional force of such a still image is a way into a writing task from alternative viewpoints. These perspectives may be written in prose, spoken as monologues, or produced as poems. Small group still images depicting bullying may be presented as though they are slides shown on a screen at a conference for teachers on bullying.

Thought Tracking

Here children are invited to express the thoughts of characters. It is most interesting when there is some complexity in the thoughts, or a contrast between what the character is presenting on the outside and thinking inside. Thought tracking is a reflective activity encouraging children to probe beneath the surface. It helps them to understand subtext in literary text. There are many ways that thought tracking can operate. The selection, again, depends on the purpose of the activity.

Tip 1

Be sure about why hearing the thoughts will contribute to the work. If characters are being open and honest, then nothing will be added by hearing their thoughts. Thought tracking has many functions. Flemming uses it as a way of exploring a subtext in a narrative poem, whilst Bunyan engages reflection in order to deepen commitment to the character's situation.

Tip 2

Consider whether the thoughts are accompanying stillness or movement. This may depend on whether the thought tracking is crystallising one particular moment, or covering a decision that must be made. When Giant wakes, she sees the destruction and after a while decides to leave. Here Boshell's class spoke Giant's thoughts aloud as Boshell, in role as Giant awoke, looked at the mess and responded with expressions of sadness or anger according to the children's contributions of thoughts. Finally, she made the decision to go. When Bunyan's class thought tracked, they were exploring a still moment. Two boys are shown in a picture looking out to sea. The father of one of them is a sailor out at sea who hasn't seen his son for a long time. The children track the thoughts that may go through the son's mind as he looks out to sea. No movement is used here. It is not appropriate. The stillness supports the isolation of the boy. There is no action to be taken.

Tip 3

It is often helpful to ask for suggestions of thoughts before the activity begins. Children have the security of using a suggestion if they can't think of anything else when their moment comes. With young children, I often ask for single words initially that will describe how the character may be feeling, e.g. 'lonely'. From there you can make the shift into what might he be feeling e.g. 'He's feeling sad.' And finally move into the first person voice, 'I can't bear it'.

Using thought tracking – example

If you want to work with Romeo and Juliet, you may use thought tracking alongside words of text.

> Romeo: Henceforth I never will be Romeo
> Juliet: And I'll no longer be a Capulet

How could the thought tracking contribute to the work? Exploring the thoughts behind these words will lead to a greater understanding of the text and raise awareness of subtext. In terms of the plot, thought tracking may enable children to see the significance of these words. For it is at this point of denial that Romeo and Juliet are declaring their love for each other, but at the same time declaring an understanding of the danger of going against their families. The love and fears of family are not literally articulated in these lines, so they leave room for the children to explore possibilities.

Should there be any action with the thoughts? It would be effective to have Romeo and Juliet standing opposite each other, slightly apart, but holding hands while children speak their thoughts. You may ask the children to decide how they want the characters to stand, and whether they want some movement. My instinct would be to ask the two characters to start apart, then walk very slowly one step each in turn. Half the class could stand behind Romeo and half behind Juliet. A thought is spoken for each character in turn with their steps. At last they meet, hold hands and speak the lines.

Prepare children by discussing suggestion. In pre-drama discussion children would discuss what it might mean to Romeo and Juliet to go against their families, and how they must feel about each other to take such a step. Might they have any secret doubts in their minds? The thought tracking will engage the children actively in the text and invite them to look beneath it. Subsequent tasks could include written diaries describing the feelings after having committed themselves to each other. All the thoughts tracked could be collected and different types of language distinguished: All the imperatives, for example, 'Go for it!', 'Don't look back!' and descriptive thoughts, 'He is the best thing that has ever happened to me'.

In Conclusion

These three conventions for dramatic activity are, of course, only the tip of the iceberg. Many more possibilities can be derived from each of them, and there are many many more dramatic approaches. Starting with one dramatic activity in a week may be an easy way to start planning your own dramas. Take one of the above and see how it could enhance your next text, be it written, told or imagined. What is evident through all the chapters is a real delight in using drama and a conviction that it benefits children's learning in literacy.

Recommended Reading

Ackroyd, J., 'A Crack in the Ice: Planning for Secure Drama' in *Language and Learning*, Nov/Dec, 1994.

Booth, D. & Neelands, J., (ed) *Writing in Role: Classroom Projects Connecting Writing and Drama*, Caliburn Enterprises, 1998.

Booth, D., *Story Drama*, Pembroke Publishers, 1994.

Flemming, M., *Starting Drama Teaching*, David Fulton Publishers, 1994.

Morgan, N. & Saxton, J., *Teaching Drama*, Stanley Thornes (Publishers) Ltd, 1991.

Neelands, J., *Structuring Drama Work*, Cambridge University Press, 1990.

Neelands, J., *Learning Through Imagined Experience*, Hodder & Stoughton, 1992.

Winston, J. & Tandy, M., *Beginning Drama 4–11*, David Fulton Publishers, 1998.